Into The Stadium

DEDICATION

For my wife, Judith, who is the best team-mate
I could ever hope for.

INTO THE STADIUM

AN ACTIVE GUIDE TO SPORT AND RECREATION MINISTRY IN THE LOCAL CHURCH

BRYAN MASON

First published 2003 by Spring Harvest Publishing Division
and Authentic Lifestyle.

07 06 05 04 03 7 6 5 4 3 2 1

Authentic Lifestyle is a division of Authentic Media,

9 Holdom Avenue, Bletchley, Milton Keynes, Bucks, MK1 1QR, UK.

Distributed in the USA by Gabriel Resources,

P.O. Box 1047, Waynesboro, GA 30830-2047, USA.

British Library Cataloguing in Publication Data

A catalogue record for this book is available from the British Library

1-85078-502-3

Cover design by Giles Davies
Typesetting and illustration Temple Design

Printed in Great Britain by Bell and Bain, Glasgow

Acknowledgements

In many ways, this book is a summary of all that I have learnt during my seven years on the staff of Christians in Sport. It is a compilation of the wisdom and inspiration of many sports ministry experts with whom I have had the privilege of working over that time.

The directors of Christians in Sport, Graham Daniels, Stuart Weir and Keith Proctor, are men who constantly keep you sharp in reaching the world of sport for Christ and whose company is a constant delight. Stuart, in particular, with his many gifts as a writer, has guided me through the text and attempted to keep me on the right lines.

Not only am I grateful to Andrew Wingfield Digby for initially appointing me to the staff of Christians in Sport but also for his consistent example of being unashamed of the gospel of Christ in the world of sport.

Two American colleagues, Rodger Oswald (Church Sports International) and Greg Linville (Church Sports and Recreation Ministers), are fine examples of Christian sportsmen and outstanding practitioners of sport and recreation ministry. I have unashamedly taken a lot of their clarity of thinking in this area and tweaked it a little for UK translation!

Thanks, also, to the many Christians in Sport church representatives and beacon church directors with whom I have worked over the years and learnt much from watching them in action.

I am grateful to Spring Harvest for the invitation to write this book and in particular the CEO, Alan Johnson, who has taken time to read the book and write the foreword in the midst of a very busy life.

Malcolm Down has overseen the publication with good advice, much enthusiasm and plenty of encouragement.

Finally, my special thanks to my wife, Judith, for her unwavering support and belief in all that excites me about sports ministry. Not only has she read through the manuscript with her own eye for detail but continues to partner with me in the many aspects of ministry that God has called us to.

Bryan Mason
Christians in Sport,
Frampton House, Bicester, OX26 6PB
bryan@christiansinsport.org.uk

Foreword

Sport is at the heart of today's culture. Whether it's a bunch of friends doing aerobics at the local gym or the millions tuning in to Champions League football, even the couch potatoes can't escape it.

This book provides a superb resource for individuals and churches who want to integrate sport into their evangelism strategy – and it comes from one of the country's leading practitioners in this field.

Bryan Mason and his colleagues at Christians in Sport have helped thousands of believers to make the connection between sport and their Christian faith. As he has helped us develop the 'Celebration of Life' programme at Spring Harvest, we have seen many people released to enjoy sport and to discover a new kind of mission field.

I have often watched Bryan at work at Spring Harvest – alongside footballers and joggers, addressing seminars, interacting with sportsmen, sportswomen and senior Christian leaders. He has something important to say – for individuals, churches and the Kingdom of God.

All of life belongs to God. I trust this book will equip and encourage you to bring the life of Christ into a needy part of our needy world.

Alan Johnson
Chief Executive Officer, Spring Harvest

Prologue

If you enjoy being with people, love sport and have a heart for reaching into your community with the life-changing message of the gospel, then this book is for you. It is the intention of the author to give you the foundational substance of church sport and recreation ministry by providing an active guide for the novice and seasoned practitioner alike. The strategies and programmes outlined are not the domain solely of the highly skilled sportsman or woman and neither are they tied to any particular age group or gender. They will, however, come to fulfilment when handled by those with a passion for Jesus and sport, in that order.

If you extract from these pages a 'game' plan for reaching the world of sport for Christ then this particular coach will have done his job.

'Run with perseverance the race marked out'
Hebrews 12:1

Contents

Introduction

The local church cannot ignore the potential of sport and recreation ministry

The humorist who suggested that Jesus was a promising footballer because of the reference to him being 'left-back' in Jerusalem at the time of the Passover, was certainly stretching a point and providing no justification for local church sports ministry. However, the words of Jesus in Mark 16:15 and Matthew 28:20 where he encourages and commissions his disciples to 'go into all the world', take on infinitely more significance for this expanding area of church growth. In this 'world' that Jesus speaks of, we find sport and recreation figuring prominently and being responsible for the composition of the largest people group across the globe, where language, creed and culture lose their divisive tendencies. For this reason alone, the local church cannot ignore the potential of sport and recreation ministry as a bridge into the community and as one of the greatest factors available for church growth at the beginning of the twenty-first century.

The British church in the past has been a bit like the typical football team that plays well 'at home' in front of its own supporters, but struggles to replicate the same form when playing 'away'. Indeed, even the home matches these days are being played in front of near empty stands and terraces. The church seems to be held in a time warp where the placing of an 'Everybody Welcome' sign outside the building is expected to do the trick. To say to those outside the church that 'we are here' and 'you are welcome' no longer cuts the mustard with the man in the street. Times have changed and the church has failed to move with the times. The present generation has had little or no Sunday school upbringing and has experienced only a smattering of Christian education in schools. Together with the absence of Christian role models in home and society, a huge step needs to be taken by the average person if he or she is to step inside a church. Will this generation respond to an 'everybody welcome' sign? I think not.

Jesus the Role Model

A radical change is called for. The church is still 'here' and unbelievers are still outside the church, but the clarion call needs to end with 'we are coming' rather than 'you're welcome'. Jesus did not take up a synagogue stance and wait for needy people to join him there. He spent his earthly life out of the normal religious environment of his day. The week might start with him defying culture as he sat by a well with a woman of questionable character. It was, however, a situation that changed the woman of Samaria's life for eternity and brought spiritual revival to her village. Not a bad 'away' result for the Kingdom of God. The following day may have found him speaking to a capacity crowd on a grassy knoll overlooking Lake Galilee. Many would have been delighted that day because the Son of God came onto their turf, and who knows how many other lives were changed because of that day's work? The religious representatives would have then become apoplectic at the sight of Jesus disappearing into the red light district of the time in order to extend the love of God to Mary Magdalene in a church 'no go' area.

With Jesus as the role model for moving outside the confines of the church building, the church should be inspired to follow his example. In this respect, there is an ideal opportunity for those with a passion for Jesus and sport. This spiritual and physical combination is probably the best-kept secret in Christendom. The purpose of this book is to uncover this secret and provide the twenty-first century sports disciples with a thrilling opportunity to extend the Kingdom of God by reaching the lost with the good news of salvation in Christ.

It is my contention that sport is as vital a part of the church programme as youth work or women's ministry. Indeed, by its all-encompassing nature, it reaches out to every age group. As we move into a new century that will shortly see the over 50s age group become one third of the population in the UK, the church needs to have a dynamic policy towards both young and old and an appropriate programme to suit. Sport and recreation can meet these criteria at every level, from children to the active retired. Later in the book, there will be a closer examination of different age groups and a teasing out of the activities to suit each one in turn.

Finally, the emphasis in any local church sport and recreation programme must be on outreach. The one-off meeting with the well-known sports personality, which may well attract a capacity crowd of course, is not genuine sports ministry unless it is crafted around a regular ongoing schedule and is equally sensitive to the personality being exposed. The ideal scenario is the creation of a situation where people enjoy the company and the activity and Jesus

Jesus can be talked about as naturally as the sports results from the previous day

can be talked about as naturally as the sports results from the previous day. Research continues to reveal the high percentage of people who become Christians due to the influence of a Christian friend. Sport is such an ideal atmosphere for making friends and sharing the difference Jesus Christ makes in your life. It is arguably the greatest door of opportunity in the post-modern world for the church to grow.

As you read this book and put its ideas into practice, it is my hope and prayer that your local church will grow significantly. It will have ventured Into the Stadium.

CHAPTER 1

Good Foundations

'Remember, there is only one foundation, the one already laid: Jesus Christ'
1 Corinthians 3:11
(The Message)

To Russia With Love

I have spent some time in Russia working with Russian churches and seeking to convince them of the viability and potential of sport and recreation ministry in a land still in turmoil but open to the life changing qualities of the gospel. Unfortunately, the Russian pastors remember too much of the abuse of sport under communism prior to 1991 and find it hard to believe that sport and recreation can have any spiritual benefit. The church that had banned one of its members for jogging in his spare time would be firmly in this camp, as would the USSR 50 kilometre cycling champion of the 1980s that I met at a Baptist conference in Bryansk. Since becoming a Christian, he had not got back on his bike and described his only feeling of euphoria in all his years of cycling as lasting about thirty seconds. That was when he stood on the podium to receive his medal. The rest he recalled as being a waste of time when he was a slave to the idol of sport. I am pleased to say that the resultant conversations and later email correspondence that we had served to reveal to Vladimir the incredible gifting he had received from God and how he could use it to glorify his Creator and communicate the good news of Jesus. The church militant in Russia is at a very exciting stage, and the following biblical foundations and apologetics of sports ministry are as much for them as for the British church.

Definition

It is important that we define and describe sports ministry before we seek to defend it in the plans and purposes of God. Sport is a comprehensive and inclusive term that identifies a vast array of activities with varying degrees of intensity and competition. In his book, *More than Champions*, Stuart Weir records the findings of the Council of Europe and Sport England:

> *'Sport means all forms of physical activity, which through casual or organized participation, aim at expressing or improving physical fitness and mental well being, forming social relationships or obtaining results in competition at all levels'.* (Council of Europe)

Sport England categorizes sport into four areas:

1. Competitive sport (e.g. rugby, basketball, badminton)
2. Physical recreation (non-competitive activities which are usually conducted on an informal basis, e.g. rambling, cycling, sailing)

3. Aesthetic activities (e.g. movement and dance)
4. Conditioning activities (those engaged in primarily for health and fitness benefits, e.g. aerobics, weight training, exercise to music).

Sport is gender-, age- and ability-inclusive, ranging from young children to the retired and from the elite to the disabled. It can be varied in intensity from highly competitive to instructional and activity varied from team sports to wilderness activities. Sports ministry takes this broad base and, by means of varied activities, seeks to serve the purposes of God as he builds his church through the redeeming death of his Son. It provides stimulation to those wishing to use their physical talent for God's glory and the extension of his Kingdom, as well as a motivation towards personal witnessing in the sports arena. Out of this mix may come the missionary, the sports minister, the lay leader and the effective witness for Jesus Christ.

Muscular Christianity

This was a term birthed in the nineteenth century that sought to combine vigour and robustness with a strong commitment to living the Christian life with every sinew and fibre. The improvement of many aspects of society, as well as the production of a vibrant church, were seen to be immediate spin-offs from this movement that gathered pace on both sides of the Atlantic. It was, however, in the writings of two English authors, Charles Kingsley and Thomas Hughes, that the concept was first born. Hughes, in particular, though probably influenced by Kingsley, used strong muscular Christian ideas in his internationally known books, *Tom Brown's Schooldays* and *Tom Brown in Oxford*, emphasizing regularly the powerful combination in one person, Tom

Brown, of manliness, morality and spirituality. Kingsley drove home the point in 1874 with the publication of *Health and Education*. In it, he listed the many virtues that can come from the playing of games and which no book could teach. His list included daring, endurance, honour, fairness, self-control and commending the success of others. Little did Kingsley know that within a decade a sporting English family would serve to illustrate many of his assertions.

The Cricketing Studds

The Studd family earned its place in the Muscular Christian movement when all three of Edward Studd's sons became Christians and captains of cricket during their time at Cambridge University. Charles (C.T.), in his short time in the England team, was a stunning all rounder of the Ian Botham mould, at a time when English cricket ruled the world. He came back from a Test series in Australia in 1885 only to find his brother George (G.B.) seriously ill. For Charles at that time the words of I Timothy 4:8 seemed particularly significant:

> *'For physical training is of some value, but godliness has value for all things, holding promise for both the present life and the life to come'.*

His brother's illness put life into perspective and within a short period of time C.T. had retired from international cricket, much to the consternation of both selectors and supporters alike. Instead, he prepared himself to go as a member of the 'Cambridge Seven' to China on missionary duty. C.T. had become, in a matter of a few years, the first muscular Christian to gain national and international recognition as both an evangelical Christian and an outstanding sportsman. One is tempted to feel disappointed at C.T.'s removal from the international cricketing stage, knowing the influence his faith could have brought to bear. However, as the story unfolds, it is worth noting that the verse from 1 Timothy says 'some value' not 'no value' and Charles was at pains to write home to his brothers, evoking them to both enjoy their sport and give thanks to Jesus for their giftings. Indeed, C.T. himself was able to join a cricket tour to India in 1904 where he had gone on missionary service. The tour enabled him to 'play for the glory of God' and make use of the opportunities to meet with soldiers in different parts of the subcontinent and share his faith. His ability and fame meant that large crowds were always keen to hear about his life story and many responded to the call of salvation.

The Studds in the USA

The link between the Studd family and the USA was always a strong one, from the time of Edward Studd's conversion through the D.L. Moody campaigns. When Charles dispersed his personal fortune prior to his departure for China, a good portion of this went to Moody for evangelical purposes, and Kyneston Studd (J.E.K.) responded to Moody's invitation to tour American colleges and talk about his sport and his faith. Indeed, most of the 'Cambridge Seven' became Christians through the influence and preaching of Moody who saw the value of reaching the sporting subculture by being involved in all that went on there. Such was his competitiveness, that any cricket game he played in usually included one of the Studd boys in his team so that the chances of victory were measurably improved.

The many spin-offs to this partnership between the Studds and Moody helped forge even stronger ties between evangelical Christianity and sport. Out of this engagement came the founding of the Student Volunteer Movement (SVM) and the greater emphasis in the YMCA movement on the role of sport for reaching the youth of America. It had, indeed, been a significant day in 1877 when Edward Studd, a wealthy English tea planter, trusted Christ at one of Moody's revival campaigns. Both men, in their own right, became history makers in the embryonic days of sports ministry in England and America.

Emergence of Church Sports Ministry

It was in the twentieth century when the modern movement of sports ministry really got underway. A political leader in Taiwan, after the Second World War, contacted a Christian basketball group in the USA and invited them over to coach their sport and share their faith. Shortly after this, in 1954, the organization 'Fellowship of Christian Athletes' (FCA) was birthed, starting initially as an American camp ministry for young people. Other sports ministries followed, in particular, what is now the largest international sports ministry, 'Athletes in Action' (AIA). The emphasis in these early days was plainly with high profile athletes, students on university campuses and amongst the youth. It was only in the second half of the century that the public's consuming interest in sport led to the realization that sports ministry, in the context of the local church, was a vast untapped field. As with their ministry to high profile athletes it was the organizations in the USA that also led the way in this new phenomenon.

The Local Church – God's Bottom Line

God's plan for man's salvation in Christ has not deviated since the first century, when a mixed bunch of individuals waited in Jerusalem for the promise that would rock the world – the coming of the Holy Spirit. The fellowship of believers, known later as the local church, became Heaven's mechanism for change and the medium through which God proclaims his free gift of eternal life through faith in his son Jesus. This local church needs to be a solid and effective part of the local community, role-modelling the Kingdom of God to a world that is perishing in its own selfishness. It needs to adapt to cultural changes and constantly have an eye on where people are to be found and what their needs are. In a sentence, the local church is ready made for sports evangelism.

In a sentence, the local church is ready made for sports evangelism

UK Expansion

In 1993, Christians in Sport invited Rodger Oswald of Church Sports International (CSI) to leave the sunshine state of California for a short while in order to visit the UK with the express purpose of stimulating the organization into considering the development of a new department, 'Church Sport and Recreation Ministry'. Christians in Sport wanted to be an active resource to churches already involved in sports ministry as well as those wanting to know how they could start.

Edward Studd and D.L. Moody would have been proud of the continuation of the plan they had set in motion a century or so earlier.

Rodger toured the major cities as well as being the keynote speaker at Christians in Sport's national conference in Shropshire. The author found himself at that conference as a volunteer worker with Christians in Sport but also masquerading as a deputy headmaster from a Yorkshire comprehensive school. Through God's leading and Rodger's ministry that weekend, a series of events were set in motion. Christians in Sport advertised the post of national co-ordinator for church sports ministry and I was appointed.

Coming out of teaching after thirty years was a big decision, especially since Garforth Community College, where I had taught for the previous sixteen years, was a flagship for the Leeds Authority in so many ways. I had spent many occasions at the Civic Hall in Leeds listening to parents, whose children were on an extensive waiting list, giving their reasons why they were anxious for their child to be awarded a place at GCC. For most of my time at Garforth, the school had been piloted by Lawrie Lowton who had gained an OBE for his exceptional service to Education in Leeds. Lawrie's challenging Christian faith and leadership made working at the College a real privilege and, being part of the management team, a real challenge. As one whose advice I value above all others, his support for our new venture was both encouraging and unwavering. He continues to be a strong supporter of the work Judith and I do and of Christians in Sport as an organization.

God's Command

The church of Jesus Christ has been issued with a clear commission from its founder. It is to '*preach the good news to all creation*' (Mark 16:15) at any and every opportunity, wherever people are gathered. Jesus had role modelled this principle before crowds in the synagogue and also at weddings, funerals and on the hillsides of Galilee.

In an age when people gather in their thousands at leisure clubs, stadiums, aerobic studios, fun runs and golf clubs, it becomes vital for those Christians found naturally in these areas to live the Christian life and tell their story to their friends.

We are commanded further to proclaim '*forgiveness of sins*' (Luke 24:47). In the intense cauldron of sport, how readily self-interest and self-importance take centre stage and little thought is given to the plight or otherwise of one's opponent. The situation can easily become gladiatorial rather than attaining the true meaning of competition which is 'to strive together' or, in the words of the Olympic ideal, 'it's not the winning it's the taking part' (Baron Pierre de Coubertin). The sporting Christian demonstrates true sportsmanship when he or she can role model the truth of Ephesians 4:32 – 'be kind and compassionate to one another, forgiving each other, just as in Christ God forgave you'. What a privilege to demonstrate God's gift of forgiveness in the arena of sport. Those of you who have had some intense situations in this arena will know what I mean when I describe it as a gift, heaven-sent.

Another vital aspect of God's command to the church is to '*make disciples*' (Matthew 28:19). The very nature of sport with its strong relational connotation offers enormous potential as a Christ-centred environment. There is a potential to teach, train and transmit on a regular and ongoing basis. No finer example, as I work on the draft of this book, is that of Jason Robinson, the rugby international who has represented the British Isles at both rugby codes. The arrival of Va'aiga Tuigamala, the Western Samoan 'All Black', at Jason's club, Wigan, in the middle of the 1990s served to change this young man's life to the very core. His interview with *The Times* on 1 November 1999 revealed the significance of this burgeoning relationship:

'I saw this man who played the same game as me but didn't need all the going out and drinking. He was at peace with himself. There was something there that I wanted, so I talked to him about it and he explained his faith. I used to be one of the lads and was down at the pub all the time. I've

not been in a pub drinking for four years. There's more to life than sitting in a smelly pub.'

As 'Inga' Tuigamala first witnessed to Jason and then discipled him, a mature and purposeful Christian life began to develop in this outstanding rugby player. Following Inga's example, Jason joined a church and started combing through his Bible. He soon started helping to improve the lives of the socially deprived and began to play all his games with wristbands marked with a cross. The latter has no superstitious link, but is rather to recommend and glorify his Saviour in the arena where he first met him. Who better to disciple in the world of sport than the one involved in the world of sport. As Jason was taught and trained by his good friend Inga he is now confident to communicate his own personal faith in Christ at any and every opportunity as the regular media reports indicate. There can be no greater privilege for the Christian sportsman than to lead a team-mate to Christ and then play a significant part in his discipleship.

There was something there that I wanted

Sports Missionaries

When Jesus was born into an ordinary family and first visited by shepherds, it was God's way of saying that 'no go' areas in the providence of Heaven don't exist. The prayer of Jesus in John 17:18 acknowledges this very truth and then builds on it with the words 'I have sent them into the world'. That divine mystery which enabled God to visit us in human form is particularly significant in the sporting world. In the same way that God communicates with man through his Son's humanity, so the sporting Christian enters that vast subculture of sport with the same life-changing message. The prophet Ezekiel was given clear instructions to take God's words to a people who spoke the same language and had a similar understanding (Ezekiel 3:4–6). The language of sport is arguably the most unifying bond on the face of this earth.

The language of sport is arguably the most unifying bond on the face of this earth

Unfortunately, the church equates mission with foreign lands and ministry in a different culture. While not denying this sending procedure, it seems only too obvious that sharing the gospel with whom you have most in common and where you are most at home has to be significant in the economy of God. Instead of the local church bemoaning the fact that one of their number has his priorities wrong because he prefers rugby practice to the midweek Bible study, they would do well to bring the rugby club into the parameters of their mission outreach strategy. This would put a whole new emphasis on their colleague's gifting in the world of rugby. He now becomes a branch of Christ's church in the rugby club and would no doubt be encouraged by the midweek group praying for his opportunities to share with team-mates the difference Jesus can make in their lives. Members of the church turning up to watch games and relate to the rugby club fraternity would equally serve to expand the influence of God's Kingdom in that particular community.

It is unfortunate that the common conception of sports ministry is that of well-known athletes drawing a crowd to a church function, sports dinner or crusade. The erroneous belief is that they should be 'sent' around the country advancing the gospel by their fame and popularity. It is to the credit of the Christians in Sport organization that they refuse to abuse their strong relationships with high profile athletes by behaving in such a way. They believe their God-given role to be one of support for the athlete in the very area where their gifting and anointing have placed them, amongst their team-mates and opponents. Here is the 'sent' area, their 'Jerusalem, Judea, Samaria and the ends of the earth' (Acts 1:8).

The Church Team

For many years now Rodger Oswald, of Church Sports International, has advocated that a travelling sports team should be the natural outgrowth of a sports ministry or a discipleship training programme that has taken time to train the athlete as well as develop his ministry gifts. Rodger believes this can begin with such a team playing in a church league and including in their training programme Bible study sessions that explore the individual's standing in Christ and how they can use their talents to serve him. The next step may be to join a secular league with the high priority of sharing their faith through competition in a more hostile environment. Bible studies under these circumstances would include such topics as how to give your testimony, share the gospel in a sports setting and develop relationships. Coming under scrutiny would be the progress made in 'walking the walk' on the field of play as well as 'talking the talk'. It would not be a quantum leap from this situation for the team to then begin to visit detention centres and prisons to both play and share their faith with the inmates. The team may finally plan an overseas venture with the express purpose of supporting and encouraging the local church to reach out to its community through the medium of sport. In 1997, while in California, I met with Jim Urbanovich, the Sports Pastor at Emmanuel Church, Los

Angeles. As well as running a very full and productive sport and recreation programme, Jim had taken the church's Men's Basketball team on a ten-day tour in Brazil. Over that period, they had played in front of 25,000 people, sharing their testimonies during the half-time intervals. Many of the spectators became Christians and many others were put in contact with the local churches.

Rodger Oswald concludes in his philosophy of sending such teams . . . 'the commitment of Church Sports International is to recruit and participate in the training and equipping of athletes so that they have a positive influence on the mission field they visit, that the life of the athlete is forever changed because of the training and their experience and resultant joy infects the entire church as they share and stimulate on their return'.

Power in the Arena

To be a witness in the world of sport and recreation, whether at 'home' or 'away' (Acts 1:8), is part of the Christian's job description. It goes with the territory and is not confined to personality or occasion. With the recent explosion of interest in both the leisure industry and international sporting competitions, there is a harvest field all ready for workers to enter with their sleeves rolled up. Gone are the days when the evangelist could hit town and speak to a full tent in the evening. Nowadays, the technological pace of life provides too many evening distractions for those who might have made their way to the tent crusade.

To be a witness in the world of sport and recreation, whether at 'home' or 'away' (Acts 1:8), is part of the Christian's job description

However, there is no shortage of large crowds, it is just that they are found on playing fields or inside sporting arenas. If Jesus commissioned his disciples to go into all the world, then we don't need a chapter and verse to convince us that a large part of that world is involved in sport and recreation whether by interest or participation. The further evidence from scripture is that Jesus never commissions except he empowers at the same time. It was for this reason that his earthly 'team' were commanded to wait in Jerusalem for the power of the Holy Spirit and then to go and be witnesses both at home and abroad.

The Call to Sports Ministry

There can be no more exciting occasion in an athlete's life than to be 'called up' to compete for his country. I remember a young man I taught, Chris Silverwood, getting excited when he was selected to play for the School Under 12 cricket team. One can only imagine how he felt a few years later when he was also 'called up' in turn by the England Under 19 side, the Yorkshire County Championship team and finally, the full England Test XI.

To fulfil God's command is to respond to a heavenly 'call-up' that can take on three forms. Firstly, the general call is the one received by all who decide to follow Christ and is encapsulated in the call for the disciples to become 'fishers of men' in Matthew 4:19. This call is not an optional extra or a special gifting. Rather it goes with the job description and should be the Christian's life long mission. The rugby player becomes a 'fisher' of rugby players and the golfer a 'fisher' of golfers. Wherever God places us is the place where we seek to

To fulfil God's command is to respond to a heavenly 'call-up'

impact the Kingdom of God and make a difference. The sports world is a huge harvest field and as needy as most.

Secondly, Paul advises us in his letter to the church at Corinth, (2 Corinthians 5:17–20) that we are not only fishers but also 'ambassadors'. We have been personally called to represent the God we serve in a foreign land. The lone Christian in the netball team should not bemoan the fact that she is the only one there, but rather rejoice in the privilege of being God's ambassador in the side. Without her, there would be no fragrance of Christ in that arena. When you also consider that an ambassador comes with the full protection of her sovereign, then this is certainly a 'call-up' to take seriously.

Finally, there is the 'special' call of God on the Christian athlete. This is the call to use your gifting, talents and positioning to advance the cause of Christ in the lives of those you are able to influence by your lifestyle and conversation. Paul's instruction to Archippus in Colossians 4:17 was very much along these lines when he told him to 'complete the work' that he had 'received in the Lord'.

Many who read this book might feel that their ministry is to be in the world of sport and that this is their 'special' calling. It is a call that needs to be understood also by the church and its leadership so that the individual can be recognized as the church's arm into the sporting world. Indeed, when the Apostle Paul recognized certain gifts in people he saw to it that they were 'set aside' for the work and equipped for their ministry. In the same way, the Christian athlete should seek to fulfil all that God has invested in him. It may be as a national or international figure, an influential coach, a keen local team player, a physical education teacher or a youth leader with a sporting passion. In all cases, the significance of this position in the world of sport must not be underestimated.

Role of the Church

The individual fulfils the command of God by responding to the call of God but how does the Church similarly respond? In a hostile world it needs to be constantly reaching upward, inward and outward in order to be the very best that God intended.

In response to those well-known words recorded in the Westminster catechism summarizing man's chief end – 'to love God and enjoy him forever' – the Church reaches upward in worship. Before gazing inward and outward, the focus must always be upward towards the Creator, who holds all things together by his power and might. In upward gazing and experiencing sheer enjoyment of God for who he is – a state that can be as significant on the sports field as in the church pew – the Christian is then stimulated to grow in faith and reach inward. The Apostle Paul provokes his fellow worker, Timothy, to be 'equipped for every good work' (2 Timothy 3:17), allowing the Word of God to determine his inward journey by being embedded in every aspect of his life.

However, if the Church were to spend all its time concentrating on the upward and inward side of its necessary development, then the Great Commission given by Jesus to his disciples on the ascension mount would be invalidated. He departed having invested his life-blood into his church, knowing that if the world was to 'call on the one they have not believed in' (Romans 10:14) then the outward activity of believers was paramount. Preaching needs to be commissioned by God, continues Paul, and then he quotes Isaiah 52:7 – 'how beautiful are the feet of those who bring good news'.

The sporting world will only hear of the one they have not believed in as the 'beautiful feet' of fellow sportsmen and women take this life-changing message into the subculture.

Just do it

The Athenians in the ancient world were determined that Nike, the goddess of victory, would remain in their city temple and so they clipped her wings to ensure her presence and with it all future victories. The Christian requires no such superstitious idol and is encouraged by Paul's rallying call to the church in Rome when he told them they were 'more than conquerors though him who loved us' (Romans 8:37).

Within the context of the local church, God has determined that his work will be accomplished. If the Church is to employ sport and recreation as part of its game-plan then certain biblical principles must be central to the work.

Firstly, the principle of divine diversity opens up the way for man to use his kaleidoscopic gifting in the sporting world in order to proclaim the good news of Jesus Christ. The nature and character of God rejoices in the diversity, yet oneness of the Trinity, and in the person of Jesus, we see a referral to many titles and descriptions. He is the Lamb of God, the Light of the World, the Way, the Truth, the Life, the Door, the Vine etc. The Word of God in creation and God's diverse ministry in the lives of Abraham, Moses, Joseph, David, Peter, Paul and many more, are all indications that we are to use the gifts, calling and positioning that God has bestowed upon us.

Paul invokes the Christians in Galatia not to be burdened by the yoke of slavery because it is Christ who has set them free (Galatians 5:1). By the same token, those of us who are called to sports ministry are free from man-made conventions and traditions. This same principle of liberty is reinforced by Paul in his writings to the church at Corinth, but with a different twist. Although he is free, he is prepared to make himself a slave to everyone in order to win as many as possible for God's Kingdom. He is ready to go into any area and any subculture so that he can openly proclaim that he has become 'all things to all men so that by all possible means I might save some' (1 Corinthians 9:22). What a clarion call here for sport and recreation ministry – to take the gospel into the frenetic and intense cauldron of physical activity and seek to live the life that Christ has set us free for. No wonder that later in the same chapter of 1 Corinthians 9 Paul remarks – 'everyone who competes in the games goes into strict training . . . we do it to get a crown that will last forever' (verse 25).

What a privilege, what a calling!

Competition

The principle of preparing someone for a competitive world can be easily ignored, if not dismissed, by the Church. Yet, in the early chapters of Genesis, we see the competitive strands of creation (Genesis 1:28) and then the full force of sin and its consequences (Genesis 3:15,17,19). Centuries later, Peter, writing from Rome (1 Peter 5:8), is mindful of the same forces to be combated when he encouraged his readers to 'be self-controlled and alert. Your enemy the devil prowls around like a roaring lion looking for someone to devour'. Paul also reminds the church at Ephesus that 'our struggle is not against flesh and blood but against the rulers, against the authorities, against the powers of this dark world and against the spiritual forces of evil in the heavenly realms' (Ephesians 6:12).

Now there's a competition to be prepared for!

As with many things, the world has turned 'competition' into something quite different from the original intention. Greg Linville believes that many competitors are caught up in and believe in the 'win at all costs' philosophy of sports. They would follow the motto of the late Vince Lombardi, legendary American gridiron football coach – 'winning isn't everything, it's the only thing'.

Paul's writings are studded with reference after reference to athletic analogies

The ultimate accomplishment for many is winning and this is achieved by 'blowing away' your opponent who is often seen consequentially as useless and inept. Such a position would have no place in a sports ministry programme and would be the very antithesis of the Christian philosophy to competition. However, it does serve to put grist in the mill of those who would wish to dispose of all competition. I remember in the 1970s dealing with a number of head teachers who had cancelled all competitive fixtures with other schools and replaced them with internal friendly activities where there were no winners or losers. To my mind, these head teachers were failing in their responsibilities to their charges in a big way. The youngsters were at a stage in their lives when they needed positive leadership and guidance on how to cope with and react to opponents in the heat of competition. They were entering a world where there would be plenty of influential people only too ready to teach them 'Lombardi rules' and they needed the right kind of role models to see them through. You see, competition is not unlike money in that it is a neutral force. Whether it becomes a force for good or evil depends on the way athletes react in the heat of it. However, to remove it from the circle of activity would handicap spiritual development rather than advance it. The final thought on this controversial subject goes to Greg Linville again with his proposal that Christian athletes must emulate Jesus Christ in everything they do, including their whole attitude to competition. He recommends they take on the mantle of 'Christmanship' rather than 'the humanistically-based ethic of sportsmanship and the pragmatically-based ethic of gamesmanship'. Christmanship is to compete in the image of Christ in the way you connect with team-mates, opponents, officials and coaches. It involves competing with zeal and unmatched enthusiasm, while honouring your opponent as you play your very best. 'Competition' needs to return to its roots, the Latin verb meaning 'to strive together': a concept that puts the principle of preparation into its proper context. I need an opponent in order to hone and improve the skills that God has endowed me with. If my opponent is on top form then I seek to raise my standards accordingly so that we both profit from this God-given principle. Equally, if I have the edge in the game I would hope to bring the best out of him as we compete together.

Race of Life

The Bible makes no specific reference to the relevance or otherwise of sports ministry, but speaks volumes in its silence. If 'all scripture' is there 'for teaching, rebuking, correcting and training in righteousness' (2 Timothy 3:16), then it seems more than unusual that there are no pronouncements against athletic activities if they are for worldly use only. On the contrary, the Apostle Paul's writings are studded with reference after reference to athletic analogies that were used to encourage and bolster the many Christian communities in Asia Minor and Rome. Paul told Timothy that he was 'being poured out like a drink offering' (2 Timothy 4:6) in the way the athlete poured out his gifts of wine and food as an offering to the gods before competing, and that he had 'finished the race' (2 Timothy 4:7). The crown awaiting the athlete in the stadium was so often compared to God's 'crown of righteousness' awarded on that day (2 Timothy 4:8) and he finally exhorted the believers at Philippi 'to press on towards the goal to win the prize' (Philippians 3:14).

In the book of Hebrews, the spiritual athlete is encouraged to 'run with perseverance' the race of life and 'throw off everything that hinders' (12:1): the latter, a reference to the athlete abandoning the weights normally carried in the hands when running or jumping. The 'great crowd of witnesses' that surround this event at the end of life's race is graphically enacted every four years when millions of people around the world witness the reception given to the marathon runners in the Olympic Games as they finish the course.

One of the most moving moments for me from the 2000 Sydney Olympics was when one of the British marathon runners picked up an injury within minutes of the start, but completed the course in pain and over one hour behind the last runner. On being interviewed, he gave his reasons for completing the course as pride in his country, gratitude for those who had helped him qualify for the Olympics, and a determination not to give up after four years of preparation. He had been given as tumultuous a reception in the stadium as the one received by the gold medal winner. What a promise there is for the spiritual athlete when he enters that great heavenly stadium and first catches sight of Jesus waiting for him at the finishing tape. A race completed thanks to good foundations in that very same Son of God.

CHAPTER 2

Why Have a Sport and Recreation Ministry?

Communicate to as wide an audience as possible the interrelationship between physical and spiritual fitness and the life changing consequences.
Dr Kenneth H. Cooper

It's Biblical!

THE BEGINNINGS

To understand the role of sport in God's creative plan we need to take a look at the book of Genesis. Here we find an affirmation of God's desire that we go out and enjoy the world he has created for us. If we are to seek to image God in all that we do, then our major concentration must be in two main areas – creativity and relationships.

In the first chapter of Genesis, we see what was, in effect, God's playground. God's excitement and enjoyment of his creation is captured by the constant reference to the phrase 'it was good' (verses 10, 12, 18, 21 and 25). After the creation was complete with the formation of man, the text moves up a gear with the words 'it was *very* good' (verse 31).

God made us last, with the proviso that we should worship him first

God made us last, with the proviso that we should worship him first. We are encouraged to take hold of creation on his behalf and enhance it. The abilities needed to participate in sport – hand-eye coordination, quick feet, spatial awareness, natural spring etc – are inherent in humankind and God is delighted when we honour him by the way we play it and the attitude we show in doing so. Jesus expressed it another way when he said, 'I have come that they may have life and have it to the full'.

It is interesting to note that the verbs used in Genesis 2:15 for 'to work' and 'to take care of' are the same verbs that are used later in the Old Testament to indicate the priests' acts of worship in the tabernacle and the temple. God wants us to see that what we do throughout the week is simply a different form of worship from that which happens on the Sabbath. For those of us excited by the world of sport, that means offering our bodies 'as living sacrifices' (Romans 12:1) in worship to God by the way we fulfil the gifting he has given us in this area.

The second major area to consider as we look at Genesis is that of relationships. Our God is in community and has always had companionship. In Genesis 1:26, we see this clearly presented with the record 'let us make man in our image'. As those made in God's image, we are made to live in community and reflect God in the way we work together. In sporting terms, this means we need to have someone to play with to make the game worthwhile.

There is a limit to the number of times you can keep hitting a ball against the wall. It is important to be stretched and challenged by team-mates and opponents.

Now here is the rub. If it is valid for us to invest huge chunks of our time in sport, then we must work out whether this is of God. If we are able to love our opponents as ourselves, as God would want us to do, then this is an area where we can glorify God and grow in his presence. To 'give thanks to God' in all that we do (Colossians 3:17) and at the same time honour our opponents means that we can push out the boundaries of our own giftings and maximize our ability to serve God. It will then be possible to become stronger players in every sense: more committed to excellence and with a desire to be pushed to the highest level. We will quickly learn that being in God's team on the sports field means that winning is not enough. It is enough to have gone out and played for God.

It is enough to have gone out and played for God

NEW TESTAMENT ATHLETES

The Apostle Paul is noted for his many athletic references in his epistles. He was fully aware of the interests people had in the culture in which he was living and he constantly drew parallels and made comparisons between the challenges of both the physical and the spiritual life. In this respect, he was following the example of Jesus, whose parabolic ministry gave high profile to shepherds and farmers. He was to make it as easy as possible for every one of his listeners to make the transfer from the principles of this world to the principles of the Kingdom of God. As Jesus moved among men and women in the places of their own security, he lived an incarnational life not an informational one. He was in their midst as 'Immanuel' – God with them – who was able to change their lives and their circumstances for the better.

The Apostle Paul picks up the same theme in his letter to the Corinthian Church in the ninth chapter of his first letter. He has credibility for preaching the gospel of Jesus Christ because he has made himself utterly available to the people as their servant in order to win them for his Saviour (verse 19). He does what they are doing and, unless it is sinful, goes where they are going. In what has become a classic verse for sports ministry of any kind he says that 'I have become all things to all men so that by all possible means I might save some' (verse 22).

When Paul continued to use such words as 'race', 'the games' and 'strict training' in verses 24 and 25, he was aware of the large people group to whom this phraseology was, and is, part of their lifestyle. He wanted to become an insider so that he would have the credibility to share the life-changing news of Christ's death and resurrection. D.L. Moody summed it up succinctly when he said, 'of a hundred people searching for Jesus Christ, one will read the Bible and ninety-nine will read the Christians'.

Convinced?

Those not convinced about the relevance of sport and recreation ministry in the local church would believe there to be a dichotomy between the selfishness of professional sport and the commands of Jesus to esteem others better than themselves. Indeed, some church pronouncements in the past have ventured to describe sport as sinful, although thankfully, those days seem to be getting more distant.

The whole area of dualism is unbiblical. We find no reference to the word 'secular' in the Scriptures, but many exhortations to 'give thanks in everything'. The life God intends us to live is like a seamless robe and there should be no sacred/secular divide. We glorify God by our actions in the aerobics class or on the games field as much as we do in worship at the Sunday morning service. As we found in the chapter on 'Good Foundations', the former activity has us reaching outward, while the latter has us reaching upward. Both complement the teaching and edification role within the church where the inward reaching is the final piece of the jigsaw that equips the body of Christ to 'go and make disciples' (Matthew 28:19).

We find no reference to the word 'secular' in the Scriptures

THE ATHLETIC ARENA

There is no finer example of a Christian athlete than that of Eric Liddell in the last century. Seeing himself as a steward of his body and its capabilities, he was also aware of the body's role as a temple for the Holy Spirit. With this in mind, he sought to express his love and commitment to God through the way he ran his races and played the game of rugby. Julian Wilson seeks to explain the secret of Liddell's success on the track in his book *Complete Surrender*, a biography of the athlete:

> *'To glorify God by striving for perfection without compromise. That is not to say that Liddell's creed was to win at all costs. Running exhilarated him and he loved to win, to prove he was the best in his event, but he never sought personal glory nor revelled in his exceptional athletic ability. Magnanimous in defeat he had no lust for victory. When a friend asked him whether he ever prayed that he would win a race Liddell replied characteristically, "No, I have never prayed that I would win a race. I have, of course, prayed about the athletic meeting that in this too, God might be glorified".'*

It's Relevant!

Tony Ladd, co-author of the book *Muscular Christianity* with James Mathisen, notes the re-emergence of the Muscular Christianity movement towards the end of the twentieth century but issues a grave warning:

> *'As we enter a new millennium, Christians are operating outside the culture they are trying to transform'.*

For society to be transformed by the Word of God it has to be first of all penetrated by the people of God. Sport, like music, is a universal language that transcends barriers of creed, class and culture. It allows the Christian sportsman and woman to role-model the gospel in any and every situation. A colleague of mine, Carl Dambman, who works for 'Athletes in

Action' in Moscow, was taking wrestling teams into Russia long before the Communist regime fell in the early 1990s. He was welcomed into the country because of his sporting ability and was then able to use his God-given talent to witness to his Russian opponents. Carl wrestled internationally in the super heavyweight class for the USA and was national champion, Pan American champion and took the bronze medal in the 1979 Madrid World Championships. He has a pretty impressive testimony and would certainly have his opponents' attention once his considerable weight was upon them! His team would also work with the underground church during their tours and, as well as worshipping and encouraging the Russian Christians, they would regularly supply them with literature and Bibles. Carl works with much more freedom these days, from the very heart of Moscow, but in those days, his wrestling 'ticket' was the only way he could get into the country and share Jesus.

Sport, like music, is a universal language that transcends barriers of creed, class and culture

RELEVANT TO YOUNG PEOPLE

In the late 1970s, Judith and I, together with another couple, were pioneering a church plant in Wetherby, West Yorkshire. We were due to hold our first service and were anxious to start a Sunday Club at the same time for children and young people. We had three young boys, and our friends David and Margaret had three young girls. The Friday evening before the first service saw the ten of us occupying a grassy area near to the church premises and close to where the local youngsters gathered. A loud and frenetic game of rounders-

cum-softball caught nearby interest and before long we had a good number of the local children involved in the game. Refreshments and introductions concluded a very happy evening and when invitations were given for Sunday Club a positive response was received. Many years later, a solid group from this initial 'sports' outreach were still part of the ongoing youth work.

I am convinced that the sports evangelist could turn up anywhere in the world with ball under arm and have a group to share the gospel with inside an hour. Sport itself gives a unity to any situation and accelerates friendship and bonding by its very rules. On a recent visit to Turkey, I was invited to join some local young men playing volleyball, and an invitation to play again a few days later confirmed the effectiveness and cultural relevance of sports ministry. How often has the street evangelist been approached by the local people and asked to take up his position and do it all again? In a country like Turkey, the least reached nation for Christ in the world – only 3000 believers in a nation of 65 million – I'm convinced that sport and recreation ministry would be the most effective conduit for the gospel.

RELEVANT TO FRIENDS

Derek, like me, was in his 'middle years', but unlike me had represented England Under 16s at football and played as a professional with West Bromwich Albion and other league clubs. He was the father of one of my pupils at school, and his wife Jenny was a faithful supporter of the parent teachers' group I organized. After they had accepted an invitation to come to our home for a Christmas celebration evening, Derek agreed to join me on a men's challenge weekend at an outdoor centre in the Yorkshire Dales. Derek's enthusiasm for recreational comradeship was a real joy to observe, but it got even more exciting when he became a Christian before the weekend was out. Further weekends of the same ilk, sports outreach dinners and church five-a-side competitions, all contributed to Derek growing as a Christian and joining our house fellowship group with Jenny. The non-threatening nature of the sporting environments had been largely responsible for Derek's entry into the Kingdom of God.

RELEVANT TO STUDENTS

One of our sons, Ben, with a small group of Christian sporting friends at university, organized a sports outreach meal for all their team-mates in the university squads. Operating within the subculture of university sport, they were up front with their Christian faith and encouraged when around a hundred of their friends turned up from rugby and hockey teams, gymnastic classes and the canoe club. They had quickly realized that you had to earn the right to share the good news of Jesus by meeting folk where they were and penetrating the culture. It was an additional encouragement when a number from the dinner signed up to join discussions on investigating the Christian faith. The whole evening was a fine example of sports ministry being culturally relevant and reaching a group otherwise untouched on university campus. A local church had helped with the financing of the meal and provided a strong link for the follow-up meetings.

RELEVANT TO FAMILY

Sports ministry helps to assimilate people into the life of the church. A few years ago, we were privileged to be present at the start of a children's football (soccer) programme organized by a church in Los Gatos, California. All morning and well into the afternoon children from 6–12 years of age turned up in droves to learn skills, play games and receive biblical teaching. There were facilities and hot snacks for parents while they waited and many of them watched and listened in to the devotional time at the end of each session. The church's director of sport told us that he had seen many families brought to faith in Christ by initially signing up their 6 year old for the soccer programme. Such vibrant mornings of activity enable the local church to serve and witness to the community in a way that it can never do through its more traditional approaches.

RELEVANT TO DISCIPLESHIP

A cultural strategy within sport and recreation ministry is the platform it creates for discipleship. The relationships naturally formed within a sporting context provide the ideal area for the mature believer to disciple the new Christian. As well as building up their friendship level, time can also be carved out for Bible study, prayer and sharing their faith with others. Instruction and accountability take place in the very area where the disciple and the discipler long to be and spend the majority of their time.

When Graham Daniels, the General Director of Christians in Sport, was playing professional football with Cambridge United, he found his position under threat from a new signing, Alan Comfort. Graham's positive attitude to Alan's signing, and a concerted effort to help assimilate him into the club and its playing strategies, impressed the new recruit and a deep friendship ensued. Graham shared his Christian faith openly with Alan and, before long, Alan became a Christian. The two men spent much time in each other's company and grew in their Christian lives as disciple and discipler. Alan later signed for Middlesborough and after turning over his knee in a match against Newcastle United he had to take early retirement from the game. Presently he is an Anglican minister in Essex and amongst his many duties he has helped to disciple young men and women from the Christians in Sport Academy and so continues the many discipleship opportunities that are possible within the arena of sport.

RELEVANT IN DIVERSITY

Sports ministry has an ability to reach where other ministries can never hope to go. As a cultural phenomenon, it provides unique access to people. I remember watching the close of the US Masters Golf Competition in Augusta on Easter Sunday 1993, when Bernhard Langer was giving his victory speech. His first round of thanks were directed towards his Lord who had risen from the dead on this day and in whom Bernhard's hopes rested. The millions of interested, not to say fanatical golfers around the world, were able to receive such a succinct life-giving message because of the golfing talent God had invested in Bernhard Langer. Such talent afforded the golfer tremendous access to and influence on many people around the world.

Sports ministry has an ability to reach where other ministries can never hope to go

There are few areas like sport where spiritual growth and maturity can be measured regularly. The intense cauldron of competition and performance quickly becomes a litmus test for the individual's progress in his walk with the Lord. Making the correct observations and utterances at the players' Bible study holds little weight if this does not match up with attitude and behaviour on the field of play. The Christian character can sink without trace on these occasions, or stand out like a beacon in a selfish environment. There is no place for parade ground spirituality. It is time for the tin hat in the trenches as the battle is taken to the enemy.

The contribution of sport to physical, intellectual, social and spiritual growth is without question. It sharpens up these areas and enriches the life of the individual. The scripture

There is no place for parade ground spirituality

reference in Luke 2:52 indicates the wholesome progress Jesus was making in these areas and how vital it is to progress on all fronts rather than let one or two dominate to the detriment of the others. To find a common denominator like sport that serves each area in equal measure can only be a unifying factor.

Finally, the gospel platform afforded to talented sportsmen and women is unique in its own right. For certain moments in their time-space continuum, these athletes can be used by God as powerful role-models in his Kingdom. The principle in force is the one revealed by Mordecai to Queen Esther in the book of Esther chapter 4 and verse 14, when he reminded her that she had risen to royal position 'for such a time as this'. So often in an athlete's life, there are windows of opportunity for proclaiming the goodness and mercy of God. Jonathan Edwards, the present Olympic and World Triple Jump Champion, is at a point in his life when his 'royal position' can be so influential for Christ in the sporting and media-driven world. It is a delight to see and hear of the way he regularly grasps these opportunities and makes it clear where his gifting comes from and who really deserves the praise. It was this same motivation that prompted Bernhard Langer to make his famous Augusta speech on Easter Sunday in 1993.

It's Practical!

Any ministry may be biblically defensible and culturally relevant, but the real testing point comes when it is put into practice. It is at this fulcrum point that sports ministry comes into its own.

It contributes positively to the mission of the church in reaching outward to a world without Christ. It takes the church out of its comfort zone and from within its own portals to the playing fields of life where needy people are to be found. The church does not have to attract a crowd since the crowd is already there, formed and vibrant. All it lacks is the life-saving message that only Jesus can bring.

It takes the church out of its comfort zone

PRACTICAL FOR OTHER MINISTRIES

Other ministries in the church can profit enormously from the work of the sport and recreation department. Children from the holiday football clinic can be encouraged to join the Sunday Club and Bible Class. Ladies from the aerobics group can be invited to the weekly ladies fellowship gathering, while the speaker at the annual sports dinner can direct enquirers towards the group that is investigating Christian belief over a period of weeks. The occasional Sunday Sports Service opens the way for believers to invite their friends and colleagues to a seeker-friendly proclamation of the gospel.

PRACTICAL FOR FRINGE FOLK

As well as drawing individuals in from the perimeter of church life, sport and recreation activities can also prevent others from drifting away. They provide regular activity and friendship for those who might otherwise be finding church too cerebral and in advance of the stage they are at on their spiritual journey. For many such individuals, a sports programme becomes the first step to re-creation in their own lives.

PRACTICAL FOR NEW MEMBERS

Bringing new members or new believers quickly into a place of ownership with the life of the church is an objective that most churches struggle with. Finding an entry level of service and recognizing gifts and talents does not figure high in most church's mission statements. Sport and recreation are the ideal antidotes to this problem.

Leading an aerobics group or keep fit class can bring the new member right into the centre of church life and relationships. The fact that another member of the group leads the devotional after 'warm down' does not detract from the valuable contribution made by the instructor who is key to the whole session. As the class develops, there may well come a time when the physical and spiritual content can be delivered by the same person. Success in one area is always a motivating force to press on into other areas where confidence is not immediately apparent. Recognition by the church of the new member's contribution to the life of the church through sport and recreation will do wonders for the desire to progress and play a positive role in the spiritual activities.

PRACTICAL FOR THE COMMUNITY

Perhaps the greatest practical advantage of a sport and recreation ministry is that it enables the church to reach people who would otherwise remain unreached. Every community is interested in sport and recreation and is only too delighted when this is organized for them. They are happy to attend events that are run by enthusiastic people with care and attention.

PRACTICAL FOR LEADERSHIP TRAINING

Leadership development within a church situation should be an integral part of any sports programme. The wide variety of activities offers endless opportunities for such development at many different levels. As well as the director of the programme, there will be a need for others to take responsibility for different facets of the work and keep the progress within the aims and objectives of the ministry.

As sports ministry grows locally, nationally and internationally, there becomes a great need for men and women to respond to God's call. It may be as the sports pastor in a local church or as a key member of a parachurch ministry. It could equally be membership of a mission sports team working in urban areas or ministering abroad in countries that are not readily accessible to the gospel by orthodox means. As the leisure industry continues to grow and with it the universal passion for sport, this whitened harvest field cries out for those with a passion for Jesus and sport. What more natural a place is there to be called of God than one where you can demonstrate the gifts he has given you and you can be in the midst of those whose real needs can only be met by Jesus.

This whitened harvest field cries out for those with a passion for Jesus and sport

PRACTICAL FOR FINANCIAL REASONS

Despite all the many practical advantages of a sports ministry, there are those who would question the possible cost involved. This is a myth that needs nailing down because it couldn't be further from the truth. It is certainly helpful to have your own well-used facility. I say well-used because many churches hire out their facilities to secular organizations rather than make them part of their own ministry. However, owning a facility is by no means necessary for an effectively run programme. In this day and age people are used to paying good money for their sports activities whether it be swimming, squash, five-a-side football, aerobics or a sports clinic. Sports centres, community centres and schools can be hired at competitive rates, with the instruction and leadership taken by church members. It would be good use of the church's outreach fund to send its members on courses to train as coaches, aerobic instructors, community sports leaders, fell walkers and so on. The world cries out for organizations to offer such programmes and is even more impressed when they come with care and prayer.

Conclusion

Where churches have seriously adopted a sport and recreation ministry, a dramatic growth in the overall ministry has followed, with the lives of church members enriched and a commitment to Christ fostered. Five key reasons have contributed to this.

1. SPORTS MINISTRY APPEALS TO THE MAJORITY

In both the UK and USA the number of people discussing, reading about or participating in sport on a daily basis is in the 70 per cent plus category. For the church to have no designated strategy for reaching this huge people group is at best ignorance and at worst folly. When the Apostle Paul visited Athens for the first time, he determined that a new approach was called for and took the appropriate steps. In the case of the Athenians, it was their insatiable appetite for

For the church to have no designated strategy for reaching this huge people group is at best ignorance and at worst folly

philosophy and religion that helped to fine-tune Paul's evangelistic goals, although he was also aware of their athletic prowess and the importance of the Athenian Games. His reference to the 'unknown god' in Acts 17:23 and his many athletic references in other letters, clearly demonstrates this new approach to reach the Greeks for Christ. In similar fashion, the twenty-first century church must learn to become all things to all men in order to save some.

2. SPORTS MINISTRY IS RELEVANT TO YOUNG PEOPLE AND MEN

Many churches tend to lose their young people when they transfer from primary to secondary school

Historically, these are the two groups often missing from typical churches. Many churches tend to lose their young people when they transfer from primary to secondary school. A transition takes place that is neither understood nor catered for in the majority of churches. It is my supposition that sport could play a major role in shoring up this passage without major fall out. Otherwise, the eleven year old disappears from view and may not appear again until he is grown up and possibly has children of his own.

Adult men also seem to disappear into a black hole where church is concerned. This may be because of the church's insistence on verbal rather than physical talent as contributions. It can be argued that the youth and men have a hormonal need to be physically active which inevitably causes problems when trying to assimilate into a physically inactive church.

Before the sceptics amongst you accuse me of wanting to start the morning service with a workout rather than an opening hymn let me qualify the above comments. Sports ministry would seek to add to the work already going on and not replace any traditional, tried and tested programmes. As the missing ingredient of physical activity was added, then sports ministry would be in place to reach the unchurched folk as well as hold on to the youth and men already in attendance.

3. SPORTS MINISTRY IS THE KEY TO CHURCH GROWTH

The chapter on 'Good Foundations' outlined the need for the church to reach upward for worship, inward for maturity and outward for growth. As God's chief instrument for delivering his great plan of salvation, the church can only fulfil Christ's great commission by going into all the world. Sports minded

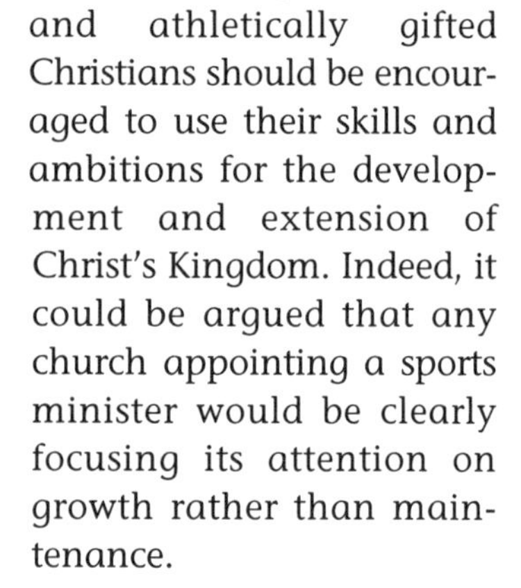

and athletically gifted Christians should be encouraged to use their skills and ambitions for the development and extension of Christ's Kingdom. Indeed, it could be argued that any church appointing a sports minister would be clearly focusing its attention on growth rather than maintenance.

Any church appointing a sports minister would be clearly focusing its attention on growth rather than maintenance

4. SPORTS MINISTRY IS CONDUCIVE TO SHARING YOUR FAITH

It is not easy for Christians to share their faith and give the reason for the hope they have (1 Peter 3:15) when they are not socially interacting with unbelievers. A sports ministry framework, however, provides an ideal setting for this to take place and is also instrumental in building up trust and enabling relationships to reach the life sharing level. Dr Greg

Linville, in his time as Director of Sport and Recreation Ministry at First Friends Church in Canton, Ohio, noted how this framework gave Christians an outstanding opportunity to model not only good sportsmanship, but also Christian conversation and values. The manner of their speech, the friendliness of their approach and the interest in their new friends were all attractive qualities that reflected the inner work of the Holy Spirit.

5. SPORTS MINISTRY IS IDEAL FOR THE PHYSICALLY ACTIVE

When people are relaxed and enjoying themselves there is a tremendous openness and potential for relationship building. In an atmosphere where stress is at a minimum, there are great opportunities for friendships to be forged long term. This can be, for many who are less comfortable with the verbal and cerebral elements of church, their 'route one' into church. Indeed their development in this area as disciples and possible leaders could easily build up confidence for other areas and soon see them leading house groups, mission teams and Sunday services.

I hope you have been able to glean from this chapter how sport and recreation ministry can be the church's most exciting venture to date. Accepting the challenge will see a dramatic increase in those giving their lives to Christ and, with this, a new enthusiasm in the church for all round ministry. Having physically healthier members within the fellowship will be one of the many worthwhile by-products of such a ministry.

Having established the biblical basis, cultural relevance and practical feasibility of sport and recreation ministry, the next step is to make a start in the local church.

CHAPTER 3

How to start a Sports Ministry in the local church

Do you want to go from success to significance? Answering the call of our Creator is 'the ultimate why' for living, the highest source of purpose in human existence.

The Call, Os Guinness

1. The Vision

For any ministry to be significant in the Kingdom of God it has to be the result of a calling and not the grasping of an opportune moment. In his book *The Call*, Os Guinness records the words of the nineteenth century Danish thinker, Sören Kierkegaard, on this subject: 'the thing is to understand myself, to see what God really wants me to do; the thing is to find a truth which is true for me, to find the

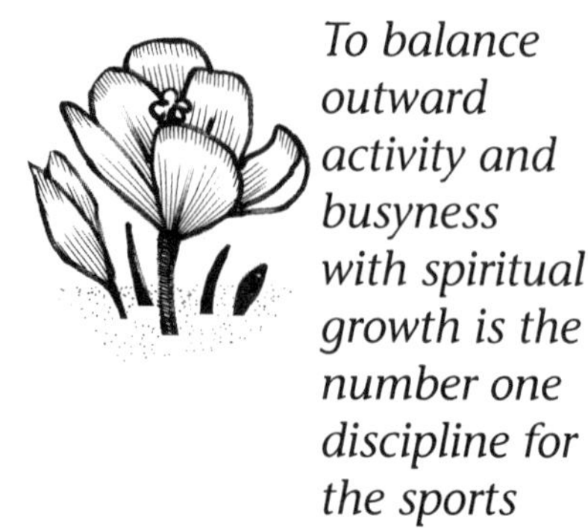

To balance outward activity and busyness with spiritual growth is the number one discipline for the sports minister

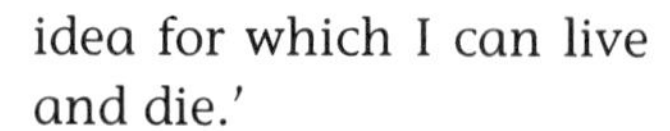

idea for which I can live and die.'

The local church is God's agency for this age, and for any potential leader of sport and recreation ministry in this setting the first requirement must be a God-given vision. Too many activities have started as bright ideas in an ad hoc fashion and, being purposeless, have duly petered out with little or no result.

The focus must be on God and his heavenly plan right from the start. To think as he thinks, we must be in close communion with him in our prayer life and in our Bible reading times. Sports people do not always find the contemplative life an easy one because they are by nature activists and energetic in their make-up. To balance outward activity and busyness with spiritual growth is the number one discipline for the sports minister. The former clamours for social interaction and frenetic activity, while the latter demands individual reflection and solitude. The two must run together, however, if God's gifts are to be maximized and there is to be no divide between the sacred and the secular.

WRITE DOWN THE REVELATION

There have been a number of times in my own life when I have sought to distinguish calling from opportunity. One of the most significant was when I was faced with the decision of taking early retirement after thirty years of teaching. Inspired by Gordon MacDonald's *Ordering your Private World* and the words of Habbakuk 2:2a – 'write down the revelation and make it plain on tablets' – I began the process of writing a journal. Whenever I felt that God had something to say to me through scripture, godly people, circumstances or inner thoughts, I wrote it down. I sometimes went a few months between jottings but then I might have a veritable avalanche of exciting words and sentences. Every six months or so I would review the journal record and use a highlighter pen to pick out the 'calling' thread. It was on the morning of 18 November 1994 that I received from God what I now believe to be destiny scriptures found in Ezekiel 17:22–24. I was in my office at school reading my Bible before the day took me over. I had already tendered my resignation to the governing body of the school, and Judith and I were still having nights when we woke up in a sweat wondering what the end of the academic year would bring. It was at this point that Ezekiel intervened:

'This is what the Sovereign Lord says: "I myself will take a shoot from the very top of a cedar and plant it; I will break off a tender sprig from its upmost shoots and plant it on a high and lofty mountain. On the mountain heights of Israel I will plant it; it will produce branches and bear fruit and become a splendid cedar. Birds of every kind will nest in it; they will find shelter in the shade of its branches. All the trees of the field will know that I the Lord bring down the tall tree and make the low tree grow tall. I dry up the green tree and make the dry tree flourish.

"I the Lord have spoken, and I will do it."'

I just love the scriptures that begin with the phrase, 'This is what the Lord says.' Such passages have my attention immediately, and Ezekiel 17 was no exception. I was appointed in March 1995 by Christians in Sport to head up their new sport and recreation ministry department in the UK, and in the intervening years I have been excited to see these scriptures unfold year on year. Our own vulnerability, the increasing visibility of Christians in Sport nationally and internationally, the growth of the church sports ministry 'tree' and the many opportunities to share the vision abroad with 'every kind' of people.

That morning in my school office was the undoubted confirmation of God's call into this exciting area of ministry. To use Gordon MacDonald's phrase it was a time of 'recalibration of the spirit' when one is able 'to pause amidst the daily routines to sort out the truths and commitments by which I am living.'

STAY FOCUSED

For the God-given vision to stay in focus we need to do more than safeguard our communion with God. We need to feel the passion for God's world beating in our own hearts as it does in his. We need to perceive with his eyes the needs of those around us as they slip away to a lost eternity. It needs commitment and availability, not merely a 'bolt-on', to what is already a busy life. Hands are required on the plough and looking back is not an option. The work is to be seen to completion and the leader called by God must be ready to stay the course.

In my journal on 6 May 1993, I noted this description of a visionary from Steve Chalke:

> *'A visionary is someone with a dream and a passionate determination and strength of will to make their dream come true. A dream without action floats around in your head and*

eventually evaporates without ever becoming visible. A dream with action is called vision. Vision gets out of your head and into your hands and feet. Vision changes the way you spend your days, the way you spend your money, the decisions you make, the things you do . . . it changes you.'

If God has given you the vision for a sport and recreation ministry in your local church then look out! . . . It will change you and your church big time. If ever there was a ministry to get the vision out of your head and into your hands and feet then it has got to be sports ministry. It is where the world is and where the sporty Christian needs to take the life-changing message of Jesus. What a privilege to be Christ's ambassador in the area where we feel so much alive and excited.

2. Imparting the Vision

So, you have the vision for sport and recreation ministry in your church. What is your next step? Don't assume that fellow Christians and church leadership are going to stand back in amazement at your personal revelation. For them to endorse and embrace God's call on your life you will need to impart the vision.

The leadership may include the minister or pastor, elders, staff and people of influence. These are the people who will 'bottom line' the work and if they are worthy of their position you will find them asking some hard questions. Foresight and thoughtful planning can only help in the presentation of your case, and considering any possible negative scenarios. If you start with the premise that the leadership likes you and wants to reach the local community with the saving message of Christ then your whole approach can be upbeat.

There may be an evangelism or mission team in operation already, so your role will be to lay out a *modus operandi* within the existing system. Suggesting a task force to look at the whole concept of sport and recreation ministry in the church would not be a bad call. This task force would be led by the visionary and would include leadership and interested members of the fellowship. The ideal time for this task force to meet would be over a weekend and if this could be arranged you would know that the church meant business with the ministry. Failing that, a day together would also give the right amount of credence to the new proposals.

3. Setting the Goals

The danger for many churches endeavouring to set up a sport and recreation programme is that they never make the link between the organized activity and the Christian message. They lurch from activity to activity under the misapprehension that sharing an activity with non-Christians is sufficient credibility for the work to progress. This can only be the case if the activity itself is a part of a wider scheme of things and contained within your 'statement of purpose.' Such a statement should encapsulate the philosophy of the entire sports ministry work.

When I was in charge of a large physical education department in a Yorkshire comprehensive school I always operated within the confines of my 'scheme of work'. This embraced every aspect of the department and clearly set out its aims, objectives and methodology. It allowed for regular reviews and appraisals of the progress being made so that there was no danger of drifting off track.

A statement of purpose is composed along similar lines and

is the directional, motivational and inspirational tool for any sports department within the local church. It encapsulates the vision, sets the parameters of the ministry and ensures that the work progresses in tandem with the church's own mission statement. It would, of course, be important to clarify the latter before beginning to compose the former.

Overarching any statement of purpose would be the components of relationship, fellowship, evangelism and discipleship. Every aspect of the statement would be located within the sphere of influence of one or more of these key components.

Christians in Sport works closely with a number of 'beacon' churches around the United Kingdom. These are churches with proven experience in sport and recreation ministry and ones that subscribe to the following statement of purpose:

1. OVERALL VALUES

Sport and recreation is not separate from the church and its other activities. It is an integral part of the total ministry of the church. The spiritual growth aspect makes it different from secular sport and recreation. It gives opportunities to share Christ with others who do not have a personal relationship with him and will help develop spiritual growth in those who are already Christians.

Two verses from 1 Corinthians, recording the words of the Apostle Paul, are key to this ministry:

'I have become all things to all men so that by all possible means I might save some' (9:22).

'So whether you eat or drink or whatever you do, do it all for the glory of God' (10:31).

2. KEY OBJECTIVES

- Provide evangelistic opportunities.
- Strengthen family life.

- Influence the physical health of the individual.
- Provide a setting for spiritual growth and development.
- Plan an all year round programme to involve all ages, from children to the active retired.

Churches in the USA are particularly focused on their sports ministry goals and the following extracts give something of a flavour of these:

Germantown Baptist Church, Tennessee

- To help reach and hold young people.
- To enhance the total ministry of the church.
- To help provide families with personal contact and participation as a unit.
- To help break down social barriers.
- To provide activities which allow lifetime participation.

Bethel Church, San Jose, California

- To teach Christian values, build Christian character and develop specific skills in the sports and recreation area.
- To sponsor and/or send out sports teams to develop relationships through their sports that will allow them to be witnesses for Christ.

Grace Community Church, Sun Valley, California

- To provide a godly alternative to children's sports leagues.
- To develop leaders.
- To activate numerous non-involved church members.

- To penetrate the secular sports leagues with a church team.

First Friends Church, Canton, Ohio

- Seek to encourage each participant who does not know Christ to establish a personal relationship with him.
- Seek to inspire a deeper walk with Christ for those who do have a personal relationship with him.
- Seek to communicate a proper Christian ethic of sport and competition to participants in our programmes and also to others who are involved in sport throughout the world.

Greg Linville, when he was Director of Sports Ministry at First Friends, could not over emphasise the importance of a statement of purpose, and believed that it should be on all communications, brochures and registrations. Difficult decisions concerning the ministry could also be weighed by using it as a guiding principle.

First Friends also communicate their statement of purpose more concisely through a motto and a logo. In a word or short sentence, a motto expresses the aim or ideal, whereas a logo gives a visual expression to the same. Some examples of First Friends' mottos are:

'Fit for the King Aerobics'
'More than Conquerors Through Christ'
'Go to Grow'
'Overwhelming Victory'

At the end of the day, a statement of purpose is there to make sure that activity for activity's sake doesn't become the rule of thumb. The establishment of kingdom goals and biblical priorities will ensure that the department stays true to its vision.

Rodger Oswald, in his booklet *Sports Ministry and the*

Church, is at pains to emphasize that before a sport and recreation ministry can be integrated into a local church there needs to be a 'careful, logical and discerning strategy' in place. To this end, he recommends that the ministry be led by 'the right person with the right passion, co-ordinating the right planning.' He continues his alliteration by then stressing the need to recruit and train 'the right personnel, to produce the right programme which is carefully promoted and diligently moderated through the right procedures'.

4. Team Building

Once the church leadership has recognized the 'call' of God for the establishment and consequent development of sport and recreation ministry, it is then incumbent upon them to set aside those committed to the vision and philosophy of such a ministry. This would be a core team with proven leadership skills and led by 'the right person with the right passion.' The co-ordinator or director would be responsible for pulling a team together that has complimentary strengths and varied skills. If the foundations already in place and the commitment and enthusiasm of potential leaders are sufficient, it may be that certain activities should carry their own sub-teams.

RECRUITMENT

The core team would be responsible for the direction of the sport and recreation programme and would be expected to carry out regular reviews on its progress. The formulated statement of purpose would always provide the backdrop for this developmental process.

Coaches and officials would be another very important group to form and give an identity in their own right. An ideal scenario would be for this group to meet regularly for fellowship and encouragement. Sharing their experiences of

Christian coaching and learning from others would be an important facet of the ministry.

Finally, the appointment of a support team would serve to underpin the whole of the work. Their areas of responsibility would include prayer, financial matters, clerical tasks, transport and maintenance. The effective working of this group would give the other two teams the opportunity to practically deliver the programme.

TRAINING

Having set all the teams in motion, the ongoing requirement would be that of training. For any ministry to be vibrant, it is essential to communicate the vision continually and make room for personal stimulation. A one-to-one discipleship programme sits very naturally in this set-up, as do regular team training sessions. Levels of responsibility and accountability are to be agreed on, with appraisal at regular intervals. Teaching on athletic and spiritual integrity would also be central to such a programme.

Some churches in the UK are seeing great benefit from sending team members away on courses to improve their coaching and athletic skills. This is proving to be money well spent from the church's outreach budget, and moves the church out of the 'amatuerish' bracket. It is always a bone of contention with me that some folk get away with slapdash efforts at church, when they must realize that the same level of performance in their secular job would be far from acceptable. It is for this reason that I have included in the 'beacon' church statement of purpose, the words of St Paul to the Corinthian Church: 'So, whether

Some folk get away with slapdash efforts at church

you eat or drink or whatever you do, do it all for the glory of God' (1 Corinthians 10:31).

A final but crucial part of the training programme is attendance at retreats and conferences. Not only is this great for team spirit and camaraderie, but external input from experts in this field gives new lifeblood to the individual and to the work, as does the opportunity to share experiences with other delegates. In fact, there is so much good practice going on in other churches that it becomes almost criminal to remain insular and even denominational. So many churches have taken years to re-invent the sports ministry wheel, when they could have easily taken outside advice and moved at a greater speed.

There is so much good practice going on in other churches that it becomes almost criminal to remain insular

5. Developing a Programme

The next step to be taken when initiating a sport and recreation ministry is the development of the programme itself. Because this is so crucial to the whole set up I am devoting the whole of the next chapter to the design of an all year round programme.

6. Promoting the Sport and Recreation Ministry

ROLE MODEL THE MINISTRY

Most churches are slow to change or to accept anything different. They need to be convinced that sports ministry works. Judith and I worked with a small chapel in Cumbria where attendance at morning service was less than twenty-five, and it dipped even more when the family with eight children went on holiday, on the occasion of the chapel's sports outreach weekend! They were a fellowship with a heart for the community, but had not seen any significant breakthrough. A key part of the weekend was to be a family sports afternoon on a field belonging to one of the chapel members. A friendly public address system, music for the occasion, hay bales, water slides and a refreshment tent all contributed to an event that saw most of the village turn out. This was then followed by a sports quiz in the local community centre and an opportunity to present the gospel. The next day, Sunday, started with a breakfast in the same centre to be followed by a sports service. When we left, that particular church was convinced of the effectiveness of sport and recreation ministry.

INSPIRE THE CHURCH

There are many avenues to be opened up if you are hoping to get people's attention from the outset, stimulate interest from all the age groups, cultivate a desire to support the programme and release action from the body of the church.

Positive promotion from the pulpit and the church leadership will be key to early impact. You will have sold the vision at an earlier stage to those responsible for the direction taken by the church, and this is now where you should reap the benefits of this. The sports ministry will only flourish if the church leadership gets solidly behind it.

When I was the head of a school physical education department, I always devoted a significant slice of my time to displays and notice boards. Match reports, coming events and fixtures, team and action photographs, quote of the week and training hints were all ways of keeping the rest of the school up to date and stimulated regarding the sports department. It was also essential to keep the displays fresh and neat so that they received daily scrutiny from those who passed by. There was a keen photographer on the staff who was happy to attend many sports events and then feature them graphically on the display boards. There is no reason why the sports department of a church shouldn't adopt a similar pattern in the entrance porch or church hall, so that the visitor is immediately aware of all that is going on in the church's sporting life.

Such displays, together with video footage, could be used for promotional evenings. Special guests, individual invitations, drinks receptions and demonstrations could all be part of this particular promotional approach with attractive offers for those signing up early on the advertised courses.

Advertising through as many channels as possible is equally crucial. Go about this in a business-like fashion and cover every possible angle. Outlets would be the church newsletter, local paper, local schools, billboards, letterbox drops, as well as special invitations to individuals. If you have marketed your activities well and they are immediately popular, you may want to deal with registration on the promotions evening. It is worth covering all this ground in the early days of your sports ministry so that the community is fully aware that there is a new thing coming.

Finally, churches can be inspired by good media coverage. My experience is that the religious correspondents for most newspapers and TV networks are always keen to discover fresh and eyecatching news. An 'Over 60s Aerobic Class', 'Dads and Lads White Water Rafting Weekend', 'Under 6s Football Coaching Clinic', 'Family Sports Day' and 'Go-karting Evening' are all public interest items that are extremely photogenic and throw up a whole lot of interesting quotes. You might even get a regular spot in some publications and this will come in useful when wanting to advertise the next round of activities.

INFORM THE CHURCH

The danger for any sports ministry is that it can become self-indulgent and start to operate as a separate unit for the benefit of the few. This only serves to fracture its statement of purpose and drastically reduce its effectiveness. Its life-blood comes from being a grafted branch of the church and producing fruit for the benefit of the whole vine. For this reason it must regularly communicate pertinent information to the rest of the church so that prayer, practical and financial support remain high on the agenda, keeping the ministry healthy and active. The litmus test would be to take occasional straw polls of a handful of regular church members and ask them to comment on the work going on and how effective they think it is.

Its life-blood comes from being a grafted branch of the church

7. Maintaining the Ministry

STAY ON TRACK

The whole purpose of goal setting is to keep the ministry focused and within established lines. We are always better at things inspected than expected and it is good to regularly

We are always better at things inspected than expected

assess the progress of the ministry against the backcloth of the original statement of purpose. Bright ideas, impetuosity and 'ad hoc' activities usually falter because they don't have this discipline written into their planning.

NEVER STINT ON QUALITY

If you plan to be professional in all that you do, then you will find that quality leads naturally to quantity. Rodger Oswald recommends a seven-point plan to churches as they seek to be at their best for God:

1. *Adequate and safe facilities.*
2. *Durable and sufficient equipment.*
3. *Kit for both short-term and long-term use. Planned obsolescence where necessary.*
4. *Integrity with your schedule – stay with dates and times first planned.*
5. *Competent coaches and officials. Where possible, train your own so they can have a spiritual as well as an activity ministry.*
6. *Parity in competition. Where numbers allow, start the course with a rating clinic and then draft the players so there is equality in the teams.*
7. *Start your administration well and keep the standards high.*

COMMUNICATION

This needs to be of a high standard within the ministry team, the church as a whole and into the wider community. Promotional evenings, registration times, team selection, schedule announcement and special events, all need wide cover through clear channels of communication.

EVALUATION

There is no place for 'inner sanctum' evaluations. The real picture will only emerge if the evaluation is quantitative. To this end, there needs to be an involvement of all participants – coaches, officials, players and parents. Only then will the core team gain some understanding of the direction in which the work is going and whether the set goals are being met. A policy of appraisal and accountability within the core team will provide excellent backup to the quantitative evaluation result.

PROTECTION OF THE COMPETITIVE ENVIRONMENT

Any church sports ministry department should have a solid reputation for the high standards set in a competitive situation. In an age when officials are frequently lambasted for their decision-making, it is important for the principles of integrity, honesty, accountability and fair play to be laid down from the start and then honoured throughout. There is also a need to clarify the way unacceptable actions will be dealt with. In this way, the unacceptable action can be met with the agreed discipline, in order that the proper restoration can then take place. The opportunities to bring the atmosphere of heaven down onto

Bring the atmosphere of heaven down onto the earth's playing fields

the earth's playing fields are endless, and must be sought after with impunity.

APPRECIATION

During a large portion of my teaching career, I served under a headmaster who never took for granted your contributions to the life of the school. He would notice when I had followed a full day's teaching with an after school coaching session, before spending the rest of the evening involved with parent-teacher interviews. To arrive home at 10 p.m. after an 8 a.m. start was quite often part of my job as a teacher. However, the briefest of memos from the headmaster the next morning, expressing his appreciation for my long stint, kept me on track and enthusiastic for the day ahead.

Any ministry, sports or otherwise, will maintain its health if built around a determination to affirm its contributors and use any and every opportunity to thank and praise where appropriate. Thank-you notes, memos, flowers, phone calls and meals out are all building blocks in this process.

REWARDS

Where these are appropriate, it is worth considering whether they need to be perishable or imperishable by nature. A trophy may be good for certain occasions whereas a ticket for the 'big game' or an afternoon dry slope skiing would suit others. For the level of awards it may be best to look out for 'most improved', 'most inspirational, 'best leader', as well as 'most valuable player.' However, too strong an emphasis on awards is not to be encouraged.

KEEPING RECORDS

Building up a good database of every participant in the various programmes is very important and can have such long-term consequences. A notification letter to someone on the books who you have not seen for a few years can prove to be very timely in God's plan for their lives. This is also useful should you decide to have an annual sports dinner and want to invite every person you have had any contact with.

8. Turning the Dream Into Reality

Os Guinness in *The Call* has a chapter on 'Dreamers of the Day', where he identifies such people as those who 'respond to the gap between vision and reality by closing it.' He goes on to say that Christian vision 'is an act of imaginative seeing that combines the insight of faith, which goes to the heart of things below the surface, with the foresight of faith, which soars beyond the present with the power of a possible future.'

Strategic planning is required with any sports programme, if reality is to be injected into dreams. The visionary needs to constantly ask questions of himself and his core team as he seeks to turn his vision into a realistic destination. A good place to start is to make an accurate assessment of the starting point, with an understanding of the resources that are available. The following five questions can serve as a useful template that will help to keep the programme in good shape:

Strategic planning is required with any sports programme, if reality is to be injected into dreams

- *Where am I?*
  Make an accurate assessment of your starting point and the resources that are available. Here – of course – is the only realistic place that you can start from.

- *Where do I want to go?*
  Always identify your goal and be certain to begin your journey with the end in mind.

- *How am I going to get there?*
  It is vital that you set your objectives, plan your route and map out your pathway. However far ahead you have set your sights, the only way to get there is one step at a time.

- *What is my timetable?*
  Be realistic with deadlines. Reasonable and clear deadlines help you to assess more easily whether you are on target. To come out with a statement like 'as quickly as possible' only serves to make the deadline unclear and is virtually un-assessable. Draw up a 'critical path' – a detailed schedule of deadlines.

- *How am I doing?*
  Many great ideas have failed because this vital step has been ignored. It is important to constantly evaluate progress against objectives and the critical path that has been established. Meet regularly with others to assess this progress. A monthly appraisal sheet can be a very useful document in this respect.

There can be no doubt that goals and objectives help our faith to flourish. Praying for a whole village to be won for Christ is one thing but setting a goal to work with young mums and their children in a tiny tots gymnastics programme and then organizing an evening fitness circuit with the dads, actually turns prayer into reality. Not only that but it lets the church and the community know that God is at work.

If you are answering God's call when you begin your sports ministry then you can equally call on God for the success of this same ministry. 'Call on me and I will answer you and tell you great and unsearchable things you do not know' (Jeremiah 33:3).

God has much to reveal of himself and his ways in sports ministry. Hold this promise before you as you explore your personal vision and consider all the ramifications of starting a sport and recreation ministry.

CHAPTER 4

Designing an All Year Round Sports Programme

In essence, two imperatives come to mind: the community has a need and the church has the resources to meet that need.
Dr Greg Linville

For your programme to be effective, it must have a long term plan written into it. This is not to say that lengthy commitments have to be made by individuals but rather that the community can see that there is something both reliable and consistent in place. It should be possible for an enquirer to see at a glance the activities running for the next six or twelve months and know what will be of personal interest. Careful planning is required if the needs of all age groups in your community are to be met.

The immediate danger when planning a programme is to be guided by the interests of the core and coaching teams rather than by the needs of the community. I'm not advocating here that extreme sports or deep sea fishing take precedence over football and aerobics for example, but rather that the planning team has a sensitivity to where the people in the community are at with their sport and recreation activities.

Assessment of the Community

A demographic survey of your community is a great place to start. Important questions must be answered:

- *What sporting and recreational facilities are already in place?*
- *What coaching/activities are being done well and appear to be well attended?*
- *What age and gender groups are already being catered for?*
- *What facilities can be hired to augment the facilities already possessed by the church?*
- *What sports are being offered by the local schools? Who are they reaching and are they doing a good job?*

Take a walk around your community and plot the facilities

Take a walk around your community and plot the facilities – leisure centres, sports halls, community centres, tennis courts, football fields, green areas, hard court areas and so on. Do not try to replicate what is already very popular and being done well, unless you have a large group that would prefer a less intense, but not less professional, set up. That then leads you on to gleaning the sporting and recreational interests of those who are already part of your fellowship.

Assessment of the Church

For your 'in house' survey to be effective, you need to consider the following tips:

- *Give a brief 'selling the vision' talk before the survey sheet is issued for the congregation to fill in.*
- *Pick a Sunday service when the survey can be given the highest priority by the church leadership.*
- *Don't let the exercise get lost in the usual morass of notices.*
- *Ideally, make time in the service for the completion of the survey. Give it out at the door on arrival and distribute pens at filling in time.*
- *Make it as easy as possible to fill in with tick boxes and yes/no answers.*
- *Collect the survey sheets in immediately after completion.*
- *Distribute spare copies afterwards to any regular attenders that happen to be missing on the day.*

You are looking for a number of key facts from this survey:

- *Where the sporting interests of the church members are to be found.*
- *What they are happy to participate in with their friends.*
- *Whether they would be prepared to coach or officiate.*
- *What technical skills they would be prepared to offer (computing, clerical, administrative).*

A few weeks after the survey has been completed it will be important to report back to the church on the results. Overhead projection graphs or a powerpoint presentation will serve to give advance warning that this ministry is organized, efficient and to be taken seriously.

RESOURCE IDENTIFICATION

Whatever comes from your community and church surveys, one thing is sure – your progress will need to be linked with resources. From the outset, you should work within these resources, and as you get established you can then start to stretch yourself and think bigger. Finances, facilities and personnel are key to your resource planning.

FINANCES

People are used to paying for their sporting and recreational pleasures, so that gives you a good start. You are not embarking on a ministry that will exert excessive strain on the church budget, so that will keep church leadership happy. However, it will be important to agree on the contribution the church should make out of its outreach budget. If we believe that the church is the only group that exists for the benefit of its non-members then this policy should go through without contention.

You are not embarking on a ministry that will exert excessive strain on the church budget

There are many ways that the core team can supplement financial support and so guarantee the continuing growth of the ministry. Coaching sessions and courses should carry an approved fee that will go towards equipment, together with the hire of facilities and officials. Certain members of the church, because of their support and interest, could be approached for designated giving. You may want to establish a '20 Club' or '100 Club' of these special people depending on the size of your church and enthusiasm of its members. Again, the way you have already sold the vision will determine the success of this venture.

Sponsorship is another area to investigate. A local business may be happy to provide such items as shirts, balls and aerobic mats, especially if you can persuade your local newspaper to mention the business when reporting on your latest activity or sports result. Marathon and half marathon runners are always looking for good causes in order to make their ordeal satisfying. What better cause than sports ministry work amongst the community.

Government grants are also a possibility for churches that spearhead youth work in the community. In socially deprived areas, the success of sporting and recreation activities speak for themselves and are seen to be making good use of government money. Even as I write this chapter, I've heard that such a grant has been allocated to the organization 'Sports Pursuits' for its work in the inner city area of Birmingham. Ex-professional footballer with Ipswich Town, Derek Jefferson, directs this organization and has had some rave reviews from headteachers as a result of his work with disaffected young people.

FACILITIES

A complaint often heard in the UK is that the church has no facilities to effectively run a sports ministry department. It is true that churches with fields and sports halls are in a small minority, but the wealth of facilities around most churches is largely undiscovered.

a) Public fields can be turned into impromptu football pitches, family fun days and sports competitions.

b) Local schools will have halls, gymnasia and sports halls that can be hired at very reasonable costs.

c) Sports centres are in abundance in the UK and even have executive suites for that special occasion.

d) The church hall or even the church itself can be a great resource facility. All too often, the former is hired out to a secular sports group and the latter handles an average of two to three hours of activity in a whole week! Chessington Evangelical Church had the right idea in the late 1990s when it constructed a purpose built church that doubled up as a community leisure centre during the week. Given the name 'The King's Centre' it became the church at the heart of the community. The large carpeted sports hall could take several badminton and volleyball courts as well as providing a full sized five-a-side football arena. On Sundays, the chairs are put in place for a worship area that takes around a thousand people. The key factor with Chessington's sports ministry is that the church has control over all the week's activities. This enables the spiritual dimension to be introduced into the programme alongside the coaching and teaching skills. Hiring your church hall out to the local short mat bowls club takes away that opportunity completely.

PERSONNEL

Leadership personnel are obviously quite crucial to the programme, and a good mix of talent and coaching skills is desirable. However, the best-planned programme won't break any records if there is an absence of participators. In this respect, it is essential from day one to educate the church in a 'you and who' campaign. There are always some who see the activities merely in place for their own personal pleasure, with a little fellowship thrown in for good measure. On the contrary, a sport and recreation ministry is chiefly in place for those who aren't Christians, in order to serve them in the community and at the same time, introduce them to Jesus. A 'you and who' campaign fits the bill nicely for these objectives. The Christian, when subscribing to a programme or an event, should always think double. Who can I invite? Who can make up my team? This policy also introduces ownership to the sports ministry programme from those participating, and helps deliver the statement of purpose. It also serves to accelerate the ministry and bring others into the Kingdom of God.

The church at the heart of the community

Programme Design

In designing a programme to suit your clientele, it is essential to be aware of the many people groups that you will have in the community: children, youth, adults, singles, couples, active retired, men, women, people with special needs.

It is with all these groups in mind that the following sub sections come into play:

1. RECREATION AND LEISURE

Under this heading, you may find that a board game evening catches the imagination or a 'Question of Sport' quiz. Both can be rounded off with a small supper and an appropriate devotional. With a number of churches, for 'Question of Sport' evenings, I have used a video of a Christian athlete as part of the quiz and then picked up on one of the points made during the video to expand on the gospel. The *Ultimate Goal* video, produced for the 2002 World Cup in Japan and Korea, has the testimonies and playing highlights of leading international footballers. The footage on each footballer takes around eight minutes and is ideal to play between rounds or at an interval slot.

2. FITNESS

This is an area where the church must have a view and a strategy. Judith and I live in a small village in Wensleydale, North Yorkshire. At the time of writing, there are two pilates classes in the village hall and aerobics classes in many of the nearby villages. In the market town a few miles away, there are two aqua-fit classes, an aerobics class, a circuit training class and a fitness studio. Those attending demonstrate a wide range of fitness and an even wider range of shape and size. Teenagers and the active retired flank this group that includes every other age group in between. It is a great place for the Christian to be and, thus far, Judith has had some great conversations with other ladies she has met at these classes, a number of whom have come to special outreach events held in the village. With regard to the local church running its own fitness classes, I shall look at this aspect in more detail in the chapter on 'Playing on the World's Field'.

3. OUTDOOR ACTIVITIES

Jogging and walking clubs provide good opportunities to spend time with people over a lengthy period of time and the activity can be tailored to suit the needs and abilities of the members. The jogging can range from 2–3 mile stretches around the town or countryside, to running as a team in a half or full marathon for a worthwhile cause. As relationships are forged, one of the weekly sessions can take the form of a light meal at the house of one of the runners to be followed by a Bible study on the 'Race of Life' (see details of this study in the chapter on 'Follow-up and Discipleship').

Having a keen walker in your church can be a real blessing, especially if this person is also a knowledgeable naturalist as well. If numbers grow quickly for this activity,

then walks can be graded to suit all levels of ability. Some of my deepest conversations with men have been while undertaking a steady ridge walk in Swaledale during an annual outdoor activities residential weekend. Such occasions provide quality time, when real life issues can surface and the good news of God's Kingdom can be shared.

An annual camping week or weekend for church members and their friends is another activity that is worth including in your yearly calendar. As well as the fun and frenzy of being together, there will be countless opportunities for morning devotionals, camp fire sharing and home grown Sunday services. Again, play to the strengths of your members and allow the keen campers to plan this kind of event with you.

Rock-climbing, caving, canoeing and back-packing are all specialized outdoor activities, but many of your friends might be delighted to participate in them. Use the expertise that is local, but failing that, you could well have a Christian outdoor centre within reasonable travelling distance. Evening talks and devotionals on these occasions flow naturally from the challenges that the day has brought forth. Stuck on a rock face and being guided to safety by 'the one who has gone before' is a powerful analogy of the salvation available in Jesus. Not that I'm suggesting that you contrive cliff-hanging situations in order to get home your point!

A final outdoor activity worth a mention is fishing. This activity has a greater number of participators than any other sport in this country. It is, of course, more individualistic than the previous activities mentioned, but the time travelling to the river or sea and then the 'après fish' occasion can all be worthwhile times with friends and acquaintances. You wouldn't find it too hard to find New Testament parallels for this activity when the time came for a devotional together.

In all instances, the key is being creative. When Keith McIntosh, one of our regional co-ordinators in Christians in Sport, found that a number of unchurched dads were keen on deep-sea fishing, he organized a dads and lads fishing trip from Fleetwood on the north-west coast of England. It was an opportunity to deepen friendships in a non-threatening atmosphere and to look to God to prosper the situation.

4. LEAGUES AND TOURNAMENTS

Once you have decided which team games, if any, you are going to include at sometime during the year, the next step is determining the form of the activity. I shall use football as an example, but in its place you could easily substitute basketball, netball, cricket, field hockey, street hockey, rugby, short mat bowls and so on. The chosen game could be played at several levels in your sport and recreation programme.

- Occasional five-a-side evenings in the local sports hall for church members and their friends with the emphasis being on fun and friendship. If the surroundings allow it, a short message or discussion could take place at the close of the activity. If the church has its own playing area, then this may be easier to arrange.
- Joining a five-a-side secular league as a complete Christian team. The emphasis now is on the teams you play, and you will need to decide on a strategy in line with the goals you have set in your sports

ministry. You may want to start and/or finish with a prayer huddle, give out sports tracts to your opponents, demonstrate the fruits of the Spirit in your playing performance and use the physical skills God has given you to the best of your ability in a competitive situation. Go out of your way to develop strong friendships with the teams you play and, where appropriate, invite them to an outreach event (they could enter a team in your 'Question of Sport' evening) or to your end of season dinner.

Go out of your way to develop strong friendships with the teams you play

- Enter your eleven-a-side team(s) in the local secular league. My advice here is that the majority of your team are Christians. Any non-Christians must be fully at ease with the reasons why you are playing in a secular league – to play competitively yet 'christianly' and to share your faith. They must also be prepared to maintain the standards of play and behaviour agreed upon.

- Enter your eleven-a-side team in a Christian league. Here the emphasis can be on the non-Christian players who should still make up the minority of the team (never more than four would be my suggestion). The organizers of such leagues should seek to maintain at all times the standards that honour God and enable all the players to express their footballing skills. Midweek training sessions should include light, but meaningful, Bible studies and all games should start with prayer and, preferably, end with prayer. The end of season dinner and presentation evening should always be seen as an opportunity to share the vision of the team and the hope of the gospel. Your keynote speaker does not have to be a famous sportsman, but does have to be a good communicator using a sporting context. A brief interview with one of the Christian players is also recommended.

- Taking a team on tour can be a natural progression of a successful programme. The dynamics of this can be found in the 'Good Foundations' chapter under the heading of 'Sports Missionaries'. I was privileged to be the Manager of a recent Christians in Sport rugby team that briefly toured Northern Ireland. As well as producing a very high level of rugby, with wins over Carrickfergus Rugby Club and Queens University, Belfast, the team members had an opportunity to share their testimonies in church and at the rugby club, as well as playing a significant part in the various community events arranged around the tour. Daily morning devotionals led by the tour chaplain, Tim Bryan, served to both encourage the Christians in the team and challenge the non-Christians.

- Residential tournaments can offer an extra dimension of intensity and deeper fellowship. To play several games during the day and then relax in the evening with colleagues and opponents alike, can provide numerous opportunities for sharing the Christian life. A magazine style presentation after the meal could contain video footage of the day, an interview with a Christian referee and a sports quiz, all before a short punchy talk from a good communicator. Breakfast the next morning might contain a 'thought for the day'.

- Five-a-side tournaments can attract many entries and are not difficult for the church to run. Players love to participate in a well-organized tournament that runs on time and is clear about the standards it expects. For details of how to plan, run and follow up such a tournament, see the 'Playing on the World's Field' chapter.

- Resources must be a key consideration if you are serious about forming a church team. Do your homework first:

- ❑ *Be certain of how many others are interested in playing and what their availability is. Start in a small way so that you can assess the ability level and detect long-term enthusiasm.*
- ❑ *Check on your local facilities, both for costings and availability.*
- ❑ *Consider the price of kit and equipment as well as the officials' fees.*
- ❑ *Form a wise management team to consider such items as match fees, transport costs, captain and coach selection, constitution, etc.*

5. EVENTS

You may feel that your church is not ready yet for a full-blown sport and recreation ministry programme, but would respond positively to the occasional event. Indeed, the success of the occasional event may cause the leadership to seriously consider a regular programme and, even later, a sports minister.

The Sports Personality

It must be pointed out at this stage, however, that a well-known sports personality is not required to make the event a success. You may feel that the personality may encourage more of your friends and neighbours to come along, but the ultimate test will be their interest in the activity and the strength of the relationship they have with you. Always work on the premise that sport and recreation are the drawing factors – they will still be around when the well-known personality has left town.

There are, of course, occasions when it is right and proper for high profile athletes to communicate their faith in Christ to as wide an audience as possible, and you may find there are times when this kind of partnership will work as an integral part of the whole ministry. It is incumbent on each and every Christian athlete to role model the gospel in both their performance and their lifestyle. They can be ambitious, and when this ambition is firstly for God's glory rather than their own then their impact on the sporting world can be immense.

It is incumbent on each and every Christian athlete to role model the gospel in both their performance and their lifestyle

Each Christian athlete has to work out how he or she can use the gifting God has given them and how they can 'complete the work' they have 'received in the Lord' (Colossians 4:17). It must never be forgotten that the first call on any Christian athlete, after their personal walk with God, is to the colleagues they regularly work with. In their very specialized secular sporting environment, the Christian message may only be evident in their lifestyle.

Planning the Event

You will do well to address the following questions for any event you hold:

- *What is the purpose of the event?*
- *How much pre-planning is required?*
- *What will be the event programme?*
- *How will I follow up the event?*

This maxim could apply equally to a large sports dinner or to having a few friends round to watch a World Cup football match. As part of a wider programme, planning it against the backcloth of your goals and your statement of purpose would be a useful exercise.

Judith and I have recently followed the above guidelines for an outreach event in our Wensleydale village. The purpose of the evening, entitled 'Faith and Sport', was to invite friends and neighbours to a convivial gathering in a village hall where Christian athletes would be interviewed about their sport and how they integrated it with their faith. The pre-planning had started some weeks before with a barn dance, at which personal invitations were issued. Good quality posters and invitation cards were then distributed around the village and surrounding areas, as well as arranging for a preliminary write-up in the local paper. The village hall was booked in good time and had been checked for seating, amplification and the heating system since it was late November! The booking had allowed a full hour before the event took place in order to cater for any last minute panic situations. The evening started with drinks and nibbles on arrival, with tables set out restaurant style to give an informal feel to the occasion.

The three guests were interviewed 'Parkinson' style and shared much of what Jesus meant to them and how he was central to their ambitions in sport. The chatty nature of their presentations meant that their listeners could extract the information that met their present needs without feeling they were being 'spoken at'. The open question time at the end of the interviews revealed something of the impact their testimonies had had on the packed room of people.

At the conclusion of the question time, a team had prepared coffee, tea and cake to be distributed to the tables and it was a good forty-five minutes before people realized they had homes to go to. There had been no charge for the evening, to ensure maximum attendance, but the opportunity to donate towards costs revealed a generous spirit from many. Clipboards in strategic places requested address details from those who wished to be informed of similar events in the future. Many names went down on these sheets, and a follow-up system was put in place.

Variety, the Spice of Life

Over recent years the following church-organized events have been brought to my attention: golf days; 10K and fun runs; football clinics and courses; five-a-side football competitions; sports outreach weekends; outdoor activity weekends; sports breakfasts and dinners; family sports afternoons; 'It's a Knockout' competition; swimming pool party – 'It's a Washout'; 'Question of Sport' quiz; sports centre activity sessions (basketball, netball, football, hockey); tenpin bowling; short mat bowls; 'Night of Champions' (explained further in 'The Next Generation' chapter); church teams in football, cricket, rugby, netball, hockey and basketball; ‘Mini Olympics’; World Cup football, cricket and rugby events – big screen showings, breakfasts, dinners, tournaments, Sunday services to name but a few!

This chapter has sought to inspire you to get on with sport and recreation ministry by identifying the needs of your church and community before beginning to design your programme. I have tried to present you with the foundation blocks for setting up any kind of programme, be it a one-off event or an all year round fixture list. The choice of activities is endless but each activity must be planned within your overall goals and as part of your church’s vision and mission statement. Should this be the case then you will begin to see a real growth in your church as your local community is opened up to the things of God and the people of God.

CHAPTER 5

Playing on the World's Field

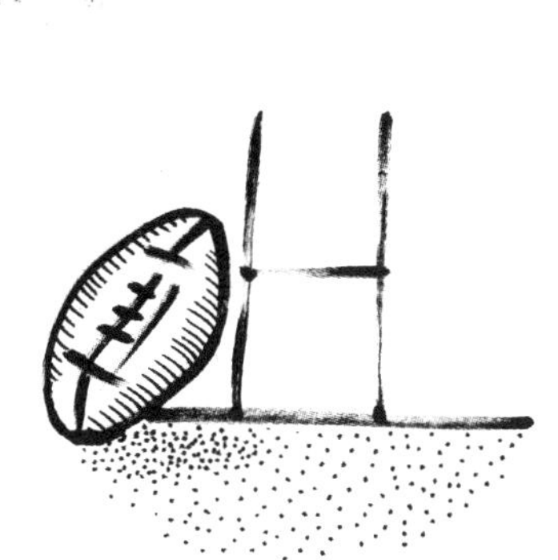

God doesn't command sinners to go to church, but he does command the church to go to sinners. Anon

A temporary measure is to give a man a fish in order to satisfy his appetite; a lasting solution is to teach him the skill of fishing. Jesus set this principle in motion when he assembled his evangelistic team on the shores of Lake Galilee. The twenty-first century church must follow his example if it is to 'play away' on the world's field and meet with people in their everyday activities.

Sport and recreation ministry in the church will have no great effectiveness if it takes on the guise of the occasional fish, used as an appetizer. I have lost count of the many phone calls made to the Christians in Sport office requesting the presence of a well-known sporting personality for the 'one-off' event. The underlying reason for such a request is usually a laudable one, in that the testimony of a sporting role model will encourage many to consider and eventually choose the Christian life. Whatever the reason, it is rare to find such an appearance as part of an ongoing sports ministry programme and in full compliance with the church's statement of purpose. It is, rather, the result of a bright idea at a church meeting or having a good contact in the sporting world. The end result tends to be a faithful presentation of the gospel to a good number of people, but with little thought given to follow-up and continuing sports ministry outreach.

Now, don't hear me wrong on this issue. It is absolutely crucial for the talented and well-known sports personality to use every opportunity to share Christ and to give a reason for the hope that is within. In an earlier chapter, I quoted the words of Mordecai in Esther 4:14b when he intimated that Esther's elevated position into sovereignty had prepared her 'for such a time as this'. For a short span of time, the national and international athlete has a window of opportunity and a platform for the gospel that will not occur again. The special gifting received from God enables this person to role model the Christian life in a sporting world that is sadly bereft of biblical standards and integrity. To acknowledge where that gifting has come from and to give God the glory for it is one of the most powerful witnessing tools present in the modern world. Indeed, I would go so far as to say that every talented Christian athlete should consider God's special call in this area of evangelism.

Every talented Christian athlete should consider God's special call in this area of evangelism

If you have been carefully following the text, you will think at this stage that I have just reduced my initial argument to ribbons. I hope, however, that you can see the difference between the use and misuse of the sports personality. All too often, the church has been guilty of a 'media' approach that serves to elevate the personality almost above their humanity and brings undue pressure as a consequence. The role played by Christians in Sport towards the high profile athlete has always been one of support and encouragement rather than acting as agents. Even at the risk of repetition, I cannot over emphasize this latter statement.

Strategy

Any fisherman will tell you that there are many ways of catching a fish and many types of fishing rod to accomplish this task. Sport and recreation ministry is no different, and the rest of this chapter is devoted to working out plans on how to use different activities to both serve people's enjoyment and present the challenge of new life in Christ. The list is not exhaustive and the activities themselves can be easily tweaked to suit your situation and clientele. All I ask is that your planning and preparation finds a place within the vision of reaching your sports community for Christ. Only then will it stay on track and not become one of many disparate measures employed by the church. Note that I said disparate and not desperate!

SPORTS OUTREACH WEEKEND

At the time of writing, Judith and I have been involved in over fifty such weekends with different churches up and down the United Kingdom and one in Russia! While the overriding aim has been to reach the local community with the life-changing message of Jesus, the methodology has varied from church to church.

For some churches, the weekend has been an integral part of their year-round programme, enabling them to invite their many contacts to specific tailor-made events and culminating in a sports celebration and outreach service.

Other churches have been praying over and planning a sport and recreation ministry for some time, and the weekend serves to 'kick-start' that into action and bring the ministry to the attention of the rest of the church. It is important that those who doubt the relevance of sports ministry within the church get plenty of opportunity to witness its effectiveness.

Finally, there are churches for whom such a weekend is a whole new venture. They have racked their brains over the years as to how they can be 'salt and light' in their communities and begin to make a difference in everyday living. In many cases, these churches have contacted Christians in Sport, usually with a high profile athlete in mind only to be introduced to the potential of their own home-grown sports ministry.

The ingredients of a sports outreach weekend are not limited to a specific age group. A typical programme may pursue the following direction:

Friday evening – the church young people invite their friends to join them for an evening of frenetic activity and an appropriate devotional. See later in the chapter for specific ideas like mini-Olympics.

Saturday morning – sports breakfast with an appropriate after breakfast sports speaker and/or video. This can be followed by a training seminar for members of the church who are either involved or being called to this ministry.

Saturday afternoon – a sports jamboree for all ages, indoors or outdoors depending on the season. Allow for a brief interview or testimony at the half-time break.

Saturday evening – sports quiz and buffet. Video extracts of Christian sportsmen and women to be included in the quiz or shown between rounds while the marking is going on. Space to be allowed for a gospel presentation within a sports context by a good communicator. This should last no longer than fifteen minutes.

Sunday morning – an all-church worship service. The style of service must be aimed at the interests of the irregular attender or non-churchgoer. A magazine-style approach often goes down well with drama, interviews, modern songs, video, brief Bible readings and short but punchy talks. All those who have attended the activities on Friday and Saturday should be invited to this centre point of the weekend's activities.

Sunday afternoon – mainly a 'chill out' time for all those who have worked hard to make the weekend a possibility. However, a debriefing session can be useful while everything is still fresh in people's minds. High on the list for this session would be planning for follow-up and 'exploring Christianity' courses.

Sunday evening – where churches have evening youth services the theme of physical and spiritual challenge could be continued. The involvement of sporting Christians would be essential here, whether by interview, testimony or talk. A sports studio or changing room type setting would put the service in a modern frame.

A number of churches we have worked with have used all seven of these weekend slots, but many have chosen to concentrate on a small handful. I've certainly found seven talks in forty-eight hours to be

Creativity knows no bounds when God is at the planning stage

challenging! Creativity knows no bounds when God is at the planning stage. A number of activities at such weekends have excited and impressed us over recent years.

Leamington Spa Baptist Church started their weekend with a 'Crystal Maze' for their young people and their friends. Hand/eye co-ordination activities, fishing for plastic fish from the church balcony, tenpin bowling in the small church gym and answering questions after a short sports video were just a few of the team competitions. At the conclusion of the evening it was a natural step to share with the youngsters about the a(maze)ing love of Jesus who competed for their lives with the ultimate sacrifice of his own.

St Mark's C of E, Harrogate works hard amongst the men of the parish with several sporting activities during the course of the year. Well over 100 men turned up for a 'More than Gold' breakfast and many took away a sports leaflet knowing that it contained a prayer of commitment that had been shared at the end of the talk.

First Presbyterian Church, Carrickfergus, Northern Ireland hired the Carrick Rangers' football ground and laid on an 'It's a Knockout' competition. Around twenty teams of ten entered from all the churches in the town and a stand full of supporters accompanied the teams. Ongoing barbeques and tuck shops kept everybody happy, and at the halfway stage, proceedings were halted for a worship band and a brief challenging talk. Over 300 people came away with a positive experience of sports ministry.

Sutton Bonnington Baptist Church, Leicestershire hired the local sports centre for their Saturday afternoon activity and adopted an Olympic theme. All ten teams, made up of friends and family, represented a different country and sported the appropriate flag and badge. After activities involving different sports such as hockey dribble, football zigzag, basketball shooting, rugby shuttle, the competition turned to athletics. Indoor javelins, discus and shot were thrown with standing long jump and triple jump as further events. Regular score checks kept the atmosphere exciting and a closing medal ceremony completed the proceedings. Refreshments followed the full afternoon of activities, together with the challenge of receiving Christ and beginning life in God's team.

St Philip's C of E, Scholes, Leeds organized a quiz evening in the village hall. Part of this was a series of questions from a Christians in Sport video on the golfing life of Bernhard Langer, the European Ryder Cup player. On the video, Bernhard talks of the time he became a Christian as a 28-year-old on the US Tour and went 'from the land of the dying into the land of the living'. Taking up this point from Bernhard, it was possible to explain to 150 people, many of whom had no church connection whatsoever, how they could progress to the land of the living through personal faith in Christ.

St Patrick's Church of Ireland, Coleraine had lost its church roof in the early 90s to an IRA bomb that had gone off in the nearby precinct. When Judith and I visited St Patrick's shortly after joining Christians in Sport, we were pleased to see a new roof and sanctuary as well as a church brim full of people for the evening sports service. New words to the 'match of the day' signature tune heralded the start of the service and this was followed by a sporting drama and an interview with a local Christian sportsman. Before the sports sermon there was a video on a large screen in the middle of the nave showing the rugby talents of Va'aiga Tuigamala, the legendary Samoan rugby player, who made it very clear that his allegiance to Jesus Christ was the main motivating factor in his life.

Highfields Church, Southampton has the university within its parish and has strong links with its students. As part of the church's outreach weekend, there was a candlelit supper for the students after the evening sports service.

Christian students invited their friends to a very convivial evening which included excellent food and service, an interview with a member of one of the university's sports teams and an evangelistic talk. Around 150 students were present for what proved to be an encouraging end to Highfield's sports weekend.

Bessacarr Evangelical Church, Doncaster laid on an activity afternoon with a difference. As well as the opportunity to play football and tag rugby, the nearby lake presented participants with a canoeing and sailing option. The church has a strong aqua-sport section and runs a number of holidays as well as the church away weekend at Bassenfell Manor, an outdoor centre in the Lake District. Indeed, many of their present young people's group had become Christians through this productive ministry. The afternoon was rounded off with a barbeque on site and the opportunity to share something of the excitement of being a sporting Christian. A sports service was held on the Sunday and the regular members were encouraged by the arrival of new folk. The church's ongoing sports programme is seeking to hold on to these interested parties.

OUTREACH DINNER

PURPOSE

To provide a non-threatening atmosphere where friendships can be forged, food enjoyed and the gospel presented in an attractive and challenging way.

PRE-PLANNING

- Identify your target group – football team, peripheral church members, work colleagues, team-mates, neighbours.
- Select an attractive venue. A neutral location is better

than church premises if the budget allows, e.g. local sports centre or sports club, restaurant or nearest league club's hospitality suite.

- Charge a price that will enable Christians to bring their friends without having to take out a second mortgage. However, the meal and the evening does need to have a 'first class' touch about it. The church may be happy to pay for the venue and the literature from its outreach budget, while individuals could have the opportunity to provide bursaries for those who are keen to bring friends but can't afford to pay for them.
- The guiding principle for attendance at such functions always needs to be 'you and who?'
- If you plan to use a PA system then be sure to have a competent person on hand to make it work.

The guiding principle for attendance at such functions always needs to be 'you and who?'

THE EVENT

- Allow a 15–30 minute reception period before the programme starts officially. This can set the atmosphere for the evening as drinks and nibbles are made available.
- A cold starter already on the table rather than hot soup will save time.
- Have quality sports/Christian literature on hand so that folk can browse through them during the reception period.
- Select a good master of ceremonies to link the evening

together. This person should welcome everyone officially from the front after the reception and then give a brief overview of the evening's programme before giving thanks for the meal.

- It is best to complete all the courses before any of the speaking starts. This gives time for the tables to be cleared by staff. It is important that there are no distractions for the speaker.
- If you want some variety to your presentation then an interview with a Christian sports person about the interrelationship between their sport and their faith could precede the main speaker. Equally, an appropriate five-minute video extract could be included before or during the talk.
- Where possible, arrange for the caterers to bring a second cup of tea or coffee after the talk. This enables conversations to take place about what has been said, as well as allowing time for response cards to be filled in.
- Remember that a high profile personality is not essential for the success of this occasion.

FOLLOW-UP

Always have another event lined up and, where possible, have details to give away at the dinner. Think in terms of ongoing ministry rather than a one-off event.

FIVE-A-SIDE FOOTBALL COMPETITION

PURPOSE

To bring friends, neighbours and workmates into a well-organized sporting environment where there will be an opportunity to play good football and hear about new life in Christ.

PRE-PLANNING

- Begin early with your planning – two to three months is ideal. This gives time for the required facilities to be booked and for the teams to be put together.
- Decide on the number of teams. Set a deadline for the return of entry forms. These are to include names and addresses, team colours and non-returnable entry fees. A good working number would be eight teams. If there is an international competition in progress at the time, then use the names of the seeded teams. Squads of seven would cover injury problems and increase your outreach numbers.
- Plan for entry fees to cover the cost of the sports centre booking. Prizes – trophies, T-shirts, sports New Testaments – could be paid for from the outreach budget, as could the cost of souvenir brochures for all the participants. These are always available from Christians in Sport every two years for the occasions of the European and World Cup competitions.

THE EVENT

- A programme of events must be visible in several areas to guarantee that the games run on time.
- Based on one playing area and eight teams, a period of three hours should be allocated. Two playing areas would cut down this time considerably.
- Arrange two pools with the teams playing every other team in their pool. The positions after three rounds would lead to the following pairings:

4th place Pool A v 4th place Pool B
3rd place Pool A v 3rd place Pool B
2nd place Pool A v 2nd place Pool B
Winners Pool A v Winners Pool B

- All games to be of six-minute duration with thirty seconds allowed for half time and substitution.
- Organize two good referees, suitably dressed and taking alternate games. If you have two playing areas, they may be happy to referee without a break, even though this is not ideal.
- A fifteen-minute break needs to be structured into the session for drinks and a short talk.
- The presentation is to take place after the game between the two pool winners. Encourage all teams to stay for the final and close the occasion with a prayer of thanksgiving.

A fifteen-minute break needs to be structured into the session for drinks and a short talk

FOLLOW-UP

It is always helpful if the participants can receive an invitation to a future sports ministry event – sports breakfast/dinner, sports service, big screen showing, big game party – so that the contact you have established with them can be maintained.

INDOOR TOUCH RUGBY COMPETITION

The template for the five-a-side football competition can also be applied to rugby with the following supplements. Book the local sports hall or school gymnasium for the evening and set up an all age and both gender competition. Women's rugby is one of the fastest growing sports in the UK today.

A few tips:

- Select sides of five, six or seven players depending on the size of your playing area.
- Play across the width of the arena and not from end to end.
- If a player carrying the ball is touched, then the ball must be passed immediately. Failure to do so gives the ball to the opposition.
- A score involves the ball being touched against the wall while still in the hand.
- Restarts simply involve the ball being passed while the opposition stand at least five metres back from where the ball is being played.
- Have a short coaching session at the start of the competition if there are those who are playing rugby for the first time.

SPORTS SERVICE

PURPOSE

To create a user-friendly sports based church service that will be attractive to irregular attenders. To make the service a focal point for other activities that may have already networked the local community and fostered relationships through sport and recreation.

PRE-PLANNING

- The attendance at the service will have a direct relationship to the activities that have already taken place and all the hard work that has been put in beforehand.
- It is good to have a core team committed to this service with emphasis on early planning and prayer.

Ideally, the service should be the crowning glory for the rest of your sports ministry programme.

- Ideally, the service should be the crowning glory for the rest of your sports ministry programme.
- Produce quality invitations and use any suitable media opportunities.

THE EVENT

- Have a lively worship programme and songs that can be easily sung by those coming to church for the first time.
- Introduce drama that provokes thought and maintains the sporting theme.
- Interview a local sports person about the balance between their sport and their faith.
- Base your prayer time around the work of God in the world of sport. Pray for those known to you in this world that God will bless them and make them a blessing.

- Make room for a short sports quiz. Perhaps youth versus adults.
- Have a sports tract on every seat.
- If you have a big screen facility, then show a video of a Christian athlete including testimony as well as performance.
- Read scriptures that bring out Christian values relating to sport and competition e.g. Philippians 3:14 – 'press on towards the goal'; Hebrews 12:1 – 'run with perseverance the race marked out for us'; 1 Corinthians 9:25 – 'everyone who competes in the games goes into strict training'.
- Present a challenging message featuring sports or competition illustrations. The following verses and themes could be used:

Mark 8:34–38 – Winning Through Losing

1 Corinthians 9:24–27 – Run to Win

Ephesians 6:10–20 – Wearing the Right Equipment

1 Timothy 4:7–8 – Training

2 Timothy 2:5 – The Athlete's Crown When Competing According to the Rules

1 Peter 1:7 – More Than Gold (KJV & CEV)

1 Peter 1:13–16 – Prepare for Action

FOLLOW-UP

- Have available sports related literature that explains the Christian life.
- Announce the start of a sports-related exploring Christianity course. Christians in Sport have produced

a four-week study entitled 'The Race of Life' that could be used at this point. The chapter on 'Follow-up and Discipleship' gives a full breakdown of this course.

- Give details of your next sports ministry event.

MAJOR SPORTS EVENT

Such is the enthusiasm for sport throughout the world that a year does not go by without a major international tournament of some kind. The Olympic Games, World Cups in football, cricket, rugby and athletics, as well as the Commonwealth Games, have all captured people's interest and imagination in recent years.

As already mentioned and outlined, competitions, meals and services can be built around these major events. Other ideas that have been successful are as follows:

1. MAJOR EVENT 'PARTY'

The lead for this activity has been given, for a number of years, by Christians in the USA. The American Football Superbowl final becomes the talking point for the whole country, and a special video featuring Christian players is produced by sports ministries, for use by individuals or groups when watching the final together.

In the same way, recent Football (Soccer) World Cups have led to similar endeavours throughout the world. As well as showing the video, before the game or at half time, the hosts provide food, drinks and appropriate literature. For the 2002 Football World Cup in Japan and Korea, a video and souvenir brochure called *The Ultimate Goal* was used extensively in many countries on such occasions.

2. MAJOR EVENT 'BIG SCREEN SHOWING'

For a World Cup football match the churches in Coleraine,

Northern Ireland, staged a special evening at the local football club. Folk were invited an hour before the game kicked off to enjoy a meal and watch a video of Christian players playing for their team and sharing their testimonies. Souvenir brochures of the competition that included a Christian message were handed out to all who attended, and a brief talk was given after the game. A local pastor had been trying for years to bring his brother to an event where the gospel was shared and was quite overcome when he turned up for this one.

3. MINI-OLYMPICS

The Olympics and the Commonwealth Games are ideal opportunities for the running of a competition under the 'More Than Gold' theme (1 Peter 1:7 KJV & CEV) and then concluding with appropriate spiritual comparisons. Several sports can be included outdoors or indoors and in large or small areas. Each activity is timed and a point allocated every time it is successfully accomplished. An ideal team number is five, although any number from three to seven will keep everybody constantly active. Experience has shown that three minutes per activity gives everyone in the team several attempts to register points. With larger teams, the time allocation could be increased. Ten separate activities will enable you to cater for between thirty and seventy young people or adults. Some examples of the activities are as follows:

- **Football**: score by side footing the ball to hit a cone or by dribbling round cones before returning to your place.
- **Rugby**: zigzagging between cones or touching the ball down on the outward run and then picking it up on your way back.

- **Hockey**: dribble between cones to the end of the line before speed dribbling back to your team.
- **Basketball**: speed dribble or zigzag cone dribble. Set shooting when a basketball ring is available.
- **Frisbee**: throw beyond a line where the Frisbee has to be caught to record a point.
- **Tennis**: run with racquet out in front of you while bouncing the ball up and down on the racquet face or run with racquet and ball and play the ball into a large container at the end of the run.
- **Badminton**: badminton serve to land the shuttlecock into a hoop on the floor.
- **Bowls**: bring the bowl to stop between two parallel lines on the floor.
- **Cricket**: throw a tennis ball to hit the wicket.
- **Croquet**: hit croquet ball with approved action through an arch.

The environmental conditions will require some of the activities to be adjusted from time to time. If you are outside on a windy day, the badminton option may need to give way to a second football activity. Frisbee throwing may not go down so well in a small, enclosed space, though it would be fine in a sports hall.

If you have more teams than activities, you can always combine two teams together per activity with one keeping the score while the other competes.

All team members keep in strict rotation whatever their ability. This ensures maximum effort from all taking part and no domination by a few.

From an organizational standpoint, the teams should be instructed to stop all activity on the whistle and bonus points can be awarded for the first team to line up straight. One member then reports to the competition scorer with their team's tally. Keeping a running total and announcing scores at regular intervals serves to keep all participants on the boil.

A coloured 'gospel' basketball can be used as a visual aid to explain God's plan of salvation

Before the awards ceremony (bronze, silver and gold medals, together with a special award for 'top effort', perhaps to the youngest team) the teams can be gathered into a central area for a short talk. A coloured 'gospel' basketball (black, red, white, green and gold) can be used as a visual aid to explain God's plan of salvation.

OUTDOOR ACTIVITIES WEEKEND

For over twenty years now, I have been joining men at an outdoor centre in the Yorkshire Dales. Marrick Priory in Swaledale is an ideal centre for establishing a balance between physical and spiritual activities and over these years, many men have deepened their Christian faith, while others have come to know Jesus personally for the first time. There is a lot to be said for removing folk for a brief period from the traffic lanes of life to a place of tranquillity in order to give them thinking time and opportunity for recalibration in their spirit. An American colleague of mine leads an annual expedition of families to the shores of the Great Lakes for similar reasons. No sport and recreation ministry programme is complete, in my view, without a week or weekend of this nature.

The planning of such a weekend should be guided by the Christian content of the party. My plan is always to balance the weekend in the direction of those who had not entered into a personal relationship with Christ at that point in their lives. The invitation letter, however, must pull no punches and make it clear that the programme includes both spiritual and physical challenges. In fact, in most cases, I have entitled the weekend 'The Marrick Challenge'.

Let me take you through a typical Marrick programme so that you have something of a backdrop to any future plans you may hatch.

FRIDAY EVENING

With people leaving work at different times, a relaxed and flexible buffet meal started the weekend off. This was followed by a 'nightline' activity on the surrounding hillside. In half-light, teams would be roped together and blindfolded. They would then work their way around a rough terrain course reliant only on the person in front for instructions – 'low branch on your left', 'deep pot-hole to your right' would be typical calls. This exercise is the best one I know for dealing with groups coming together for the first time. Bonding is swift and every individual is immediately a significant member of the group. The late night fellowship following the nightline is usually around a guitar with a five-minute talk to introduce the theme for the weekend. The experienced members of the party then know to hit the dormitories quickly and get some shut-eye before the snorers take over!

SATURDAY MORNING

A full English breakfast always proves to be as good a preparation as anything for the customary Fremington Edge walk. The morning walk is such an excellent time for relationships to be forged and new people to be made to feel part of the group. It is an opportunity for deep and serious conversation with those who prefer it, as well as allowing ideal preparation time for hearing God's voice during the weekend.

SATURDAY AFTERNOON

Here, the Centre staff come into their own, and offer instruction in a myriad of activities – climbing, gorge scrambling, caving, kayaking, mountain biking and orienteering. Each one is challenging in its own right and provides each individual with plenty of conversational mileage over the coming months. Plunging into subterranean streams below ground only takes your breath away the first time!

SATURDAY EVENING

The indoor climbing wall, mass rotational table tennis and the Marrick darts championships are all facets of the evening programme before a lengthier fellowship time. By now the group has gelled and, as well as the singing reaching gusto proportions, a number of the party are anxious to share their day's experiences and what they have learnt about their walk with God. These testimony times are fresh and relevant to the non-Christian men in the group, and the concluding talk seeks to compliment the spiritual mood of the evening. Conversations over a late night drink are always significant.

SUNDAY MORNING

The chapel at Marrick seems to have been a gathering place for God's people over the centuries. The early Celtic saints would have described it as a 'thin place' where heaven and earth come close to touching. A bunch of men in the chapel from all walks of life singing their hearts out has got to be experienced to be appreciated. The sun invariably casts its rays through the chapel windows and has marked, for many over the years, the start of a new life with Jesus. Communion and ministry combine together so naturally and few can leave the chapel in any doubt that God has turned up in style. So as not to give any scope to the sacred/secular divide so endemic in the church of today, the after service coffee is usually followed by archery and antics on the ropes course – both places where God can be enjoyed and worshipped.

Few can leave the chapel in any doubt that God has turned up in style

I have never been disappointed with any Marrick weekend, and would like to think that I will be going there for many more years to come and continue to be thrilled by the advent of new life. There may be a time coming soon, however, when the Saturday afternoon gorge plunge is given a miss in favour of a power nap and listening to the football results!

AEROBICS

It has been a privilege for Judith and me, on two of our outreach weekends with churches, to work with Rosemary Conley, the aerobics 'guru' of *Hip and Thigh Diet* fame. On these occasions, Rosemary was able to demonstrate the significant role that aerobics has to play in any sports ministry programme.

Although not exclusively female, aerobics classes do tend to attract women rather than men. In many ways, the word 'aerobics' has been hijacked, because the accepted 'father of aerobics', Dr Kenneth Cooper, never intended it to be linked solely with a particular type of movement class. The word itself means 'living in air' or 'utilizing oxygen' and refers to breathless activity that causes the heart rate to be raised into the individual's target zone, which is usually between 65 per cent and 85 per cent of their maximum heart rate. Maximum heart rate can be calculated by subtracting your present age from 220. Anaerobic exercise is that accomplished 'without oxygen' and simply means that the activity is performed without utilizing the oxygen that you are breathing. It will come into play beyond the 85 per cent mark and is another ball game altogether. Serious athletes would include a fair degree of anaerobic exercise in their training programme.

By returning to aerobics as an activity class, I shall for the purpose of this book, disappoint Ken Cooper. Should this text fall into his hands – I should be so lucky – then I would seek his forgiveness, at the same time as telling him that his series of books over the last three decades around the subjects of aerobics, preventative medicine and fitness, have been an undeniable source of inspiration to this disciple of Jesus and physical education.

Rosemary Conley's approach to her outreach aerobics class provided a good blueprint for churches wishing to install their own programme. The following characteristics were demonstrated:

- The class had been well publicized and the Christian ladies had worked hard at inviting their friends. Rosemary Conley was an obvious attraction but, in the fitness age in which we live, there is little difficulty drumming up a group of folk to join you for such occasions.
- Everything was run in a professional manner, and levels of fitness were gleaned from the participants at the outset. This determined the programme to be set. Regular checks were then made on the progress of the class during the workout, with plenty of opportunities for water intake to prevent any dehydration.

- The music used was Christian worship style that served to introduce scripture verses and understanding.
- After the appropriate cool down, Rosemary gathered the group around her and shared about her personal journey in becoming a Christian. She told how God intervened at a broken time in her life and relationships, and how spiritual and physical fitness have become God's gifts for her to share and communicate with others.

It is important that the class begins to see the interrelationship between physical and spiritual fitness at an early stage

A regular church aerobics class would also use personal testimony in its programme but a 'thought for the day' or a 'teaching point' might be more common on a regular basis. It is important that the class begins to see the interrelationship between physical and spiritual fitness at an early stage.

Many churches are beginning to think seriously about sending one of their members on a course to receive the appropriate qualifications. A two-week course, or several weekends, may well cost around £300-£400, but it would be money well spent by a church that was serious about sport and recreation ministry. It is essential that all teachers are fully qualified and that a check is made to see that the church insurance policy covers the activity. It is also vital that the person getting qualified is a mature enough Christian to be able to teach the rudiments of the Christian life and be equipped to lead enquirers to faith in Christ.

First Friends Church in Canton, Ohio, has issued the following statement of purpose and goals for its aerobic classes:

1. To provide opportunities for instructors and assistants to develop relationships with their classes so that they can experience the claims of Christ in a non-threatening, non-forced environment.
2. These relationships should give the instructors opportunities to: (a) evangelize; (b) disciple; (c) develop friendships; (d) communicate a Christian ethic of exercise.
3. To provide encouragement for those who may feel 'old' or 'out of shape'.
4. To show unconditional love and acceptance to everyone, but particularly those who feel unloved or unaccepted because of the way they view their bodies.
5. To provide each participant with the message that Christ loves us just as we are and that in our weaknesses his strength is made perfect (2 Corinthians 12:9).
6. To provide each participant with a positive experience in exercise.
7. To encourage participants to set small and reachable goals and help them to achieve those goals.
8. To provide this service to the community regardless of a person's race, creed, age or church background.

Also worthy of note are two further statements from the same aerobics programme:

1. IMPLEMENTATION OF AEROBIC MINISTRY

Fitness clubs everywhere are crowded and growing. Aerobics is not a passing fad, but part of life for many people. The fitness industry is rapidly changing by offering fresh and innovating styles. A church fitness ministry would be appealing by offering an up-to-date professional programme. The fellowship offered would set it apart from other fitness clubs. An aerobics ministry is a great outreach. To those who want to be healthy, both physically and spiritually, it offers a safe and non-competitive place to work out. More importantly, a Christian aerobics class has a life-changing message to share.

2. SCREENING PARTICIPANTS

One of the greatest challenges to the aerobics instructor is to work effectively with different fitness and skill levels. The most effective teachers are those who are able to individualize workouts to challenge class members at their own level of fitness. To best determine specific fitness levels have the participant fill out a medical screening form. Take time before class to interview the participant to determine the fitness condition. Be familiar with special medical precautions for any individual that may be participating with a chronic or temporary condition. It is at this time that the instructor may feel it is necessary to warn against participation in class until the member has their doctor's permission. The instructor may request written permission from the doctor.

USEFUL INFORMATION

The Register of Exercise Professionals (REPs) is a new self-regulating body for instructors, coaches and teachers, which seeks to raise standards in the health and fitness industry (Tel: +44 (0)20 8686 6464, web: www.exerciseregister.org). Fitness Professionals (FitPro) can also be a good source of information on training, music and insurance (Tel: +44

(0)870 513 3434, web: www.fitpro.com). The Fitness Industry Association (FIA) may also be able to help give general information or point people in the right directions (Tel: +44 (0)20 7298 6730, web: www.fia.org.uk).

QUALIFICATIONS AND INSURANCE

To be a qualified aerobics instructor you need to go on an Exercise to Music (ETM) course. The most well-known courses are accredited by YMCA (Tel: +44 (0)20 7343 1850, web: www.ymcaafit.org) or OCR (Oxford, Cambridge and RSA awarding bodies (Tel: +44 (0)207 256 7819, web: www.ocr.org.uk)

Depending on how quickly you want to get qualified, the course can be completed in a number of different formats. For example, the YMCA course runs over (i) two weeks intensive; (ii) one week and four weekends; (iii) five weekends; (iv) six weekends.

Other organizations running accredited qualifications include Premier Training International (two week intensive only) – Tel: +44 (0)1225 353535, web: www.premier global.co.uk and 20:20 Training (combination of home study and workshop days) – Tel: +44 (0)1623 827962, web: www.20-20training.co.uk. Often local colleges of higher education run Exercise to Music courses as evening and weekend courses, so it can be worth phoning around.

It should be pointed out that obtaining the ETM qualification is not easy and will take a lot of practice and preparation outside of scheduled sessions. It is also not cheap! The courses outlined above are currently ranging from £425–£680 depending on the amount of input you receive as you train.

MUSIC LICENSING

All ETM courses will include legal information about music licensing. Basically, you have three choices.

1. You can get a Phonographic Performance Licence (PPL) so that you can play the music you choose. The amount this costs varies depending on the number of classes you expect to run in a year. If you want to put together your own tape from different tracks, then you need to contact the Mechanical Copyright Protection Society (MCPS) for a licence – Tel: +44 (0)20 7306 4500, web: www.mcps.co.uk.
2. You can buy specially mixed tapes of chart music designed for aerobics, mixed together and at the right tempo. Telstar Fitness (Tel: +44 (0)870 513 3434) and Pure Energy Music (Tel: +44 (0)1709 710022, web: www.pureenergymusic.com) are just two of the organizations that do this. Buying tapes from them includes your PPL licence.
3. You can use music that is copyright free. This means that it is either original music or cover versions. FitPro does a number of tapes mixed for aerobics and using cover versions means that you don't need a PPL licence. This is the cheapest option, but you may not be over impressed with some of the cover versions.

CONCLUSION

This may all look a bit daunting. However, remember that the ETM qualification also covers information and details regarding music and insurance. Once you have it sorted, you are ready to revolutionize your church's physical and spiritual fitness programme.

'QUESTION OF SPORT' QUIZ EVENING

This has proved to be one of the most successful recreational outreach events. These evenings have been held in church halls, schools, working men's clubs, sports centres, village halls and many other venues. Without fail, they attract a wide age range of people and, having been the 'after quiz' speaker at a countless number of these evenings around the UK, I can offer up several tips from the good practice observed:

- Select a master of ceremonies who will have a natural rapport with the audience.
- Having a 'picture round' sheet on each table as folk arrive serves to get everybody into team mode fairly quickly.
- Christians are encouraged to make a team up from their friends, neighbours, team-mates, colleagues at work or family.
- A sports video between rounds with some light Christian content helps as a preparation for the keynote speaker.
- If a supper/meal is to be included, then this comes best at the halfway point. This should then be followed with a lively ten to fifteen-minute evangelistic message from the speaker for the evening.
- Response forms and invitations to future events can be placed on the tables after the talk, together with suitable sports tracts.
- Some churches have included a few non-sports rounds for those whose knowledge of sporting facts is not extensive.
- The winning team can be presented with sports New Testaments as well as the usual quiz type prizes.

Note that recording sporting events from your TV set to use on such an evening would breach copyright rules.

FAMILY SPORTS DAY

PURPOSE

This is fourfold:

1. It gives the family time together and helps to strengthen family life and relationships.
2. It uses competitive activities as a means of producing an atmosphere of fun and enthusiasm.
3. It enables the church to reach out to people who might not accept an invitation to church in the first instance but will have no problem joining you for such fun activities.
4. It will provide a bridge with unbelievers and open up opportunities to build relationships and open the door to sharing faith in Christ.

PRE-PLANNING

- Pick a date and facility in good time.
- Order a PA system and check its capability.
- Design invitations and posters.
- Advertise in the church bulletin from six weeks before the event and then at weekly intervals.
- Posters to go up with five weeks to go.
- Announcements to Sunday schools and local schools four weeks before the event.
- Start registering the participants from three weeks before the event.

- Flyers in church bulletin and through letter boxes two weeks before the event.
- Give personal invitations to all your friends and acquaintances.

THE EVENT

Helpful hints to ensure your family sports day goes off successfully:

1. Have your team leaders lined up before the event so that you can double check on all their responsibilities. It is essential that, from the starting whistle, everybody knows that they are attending a well-organized event.
2. The number of teams will depend on the names on your sign-up sheet. Make certain that equality reigns both for numbers and age groups. Keep families together. As the participants arrive, send them to their 'team pen' where they are greeted by the team leader and assistant. When each team is complete, a team name is chosen democratically and a team cheer invented and practised.
3. Plan your events with different age groups in mind. Start with a few events that are less strenuous and can act as a warm up to the more energetic ones later on.
4. Ideally, try to have a coach for each event to explain and supervise.
5. Keep the scoreboard ticking over with the details after every event. The team cheer can be used at this stage to maintain enthusiasm, and extra points can be awarded by the organizer for the non-competitive hallmarks – helping an injured team mate, leaving the equipment in a tidy state for the next team, having the best team cheer, showing remarkable team spirit.

6. It is often good to take a break in the middle of the event for drinks and refreshments. This would also be a good time to introduce your speaker. A local athlete could talk about competing as a Christian, or one of the dads might share about the difference Jesus makes to a family.

7. The master of ceremonies (MC) is a key figure who should keep the show on the road with enthusiasm and humour. To facilitate this, make certain that the PA system is efficient and in good working order.

8. Don't let the day operate differently from its title. It is a time of fun, not over-zealous competition. Keep on top of any cheating that goes on. You might be dealing with Christians, but some see red mist where competitions are concerned.

9. If you decide to have a 'Parent and Son/Daughter Day' make certain that men and women without children can adopt any spare children. This does wonders for community relationships.

10. Try to give out as many prizes as you are able: winning team, fair play award, best team spirit and so on. Have a chocolate bar and a drinks can for everybody at the end.

11. The way you close the event is crucial. Be sure to thank the guests for being there and those from the church who made it all possible. See that everyone receives an invitation card to church and any similar events. Particularly stress the next family occasion.

12. Bring the clean up team into operation. Don't just rely on that gifted group of people who always stay behind to be helpful.

ORGANIZING A SHORT-TERM FOOTBALL COURSE

Where a church can offer good quality coaching for the primary and middle school age group of children (6–13) the opportunities to build biblical standards into the lives of families are immense. The following is an amalgam of ideas gathered from churches in both the UK and the USA.

- Book your playing area well in advance.
- Appoint a Director of Football with a small management team.
- Train up sufficient coaches to cover the necessary skills. The Community Sports Leaders' Award (CSLA) and the Football Association Level One coaching award are ideal qualifications. Further details on both these courses can be found in the chapter on 'Beacon Churches'.
- Decide on a day of the week and how long the course will last. An eight-week period gives time for quality coaching to take place without exhausting the coaching staff.
- Advertise the course at least six weeks beforehand and use as many outlets as possible – church, schools, local newspaper, letter boxes, posters, notice boards in the community.
- Charge a realistic fee that covers the cost of kit and equipment. Allow for some of the kit to be retained by the participants.
- Divide the participants into age groups according to the numbers signed up and allocate their coaching time e.g. under 6s and under 7s from 9 a.m. until 10 a.m., under 8s and under 9s from 10.15 a.m. until 11.15 a.m. and so on.

- Allow time on the first day for teams to meet their coaches. Teams of six are to be a mixture of boys and girls and selected on the strength of the information given on the registration form or by previous knowledge of playing performance.
- The pattern of the coaching hour can involve twenty-five minutes of coaching skills, twenty minutes of playing a game against one of the other teams and fifteen minutes together at the close of the session for a Bible study/pep talk from the Director of Football or one of the coaches.

- While the coaching is going on, members of the church can provide a refreshment area for the other family members who have come to watch their son or daughter. This is a key time for the forging of relationships.
- A full-blown barbecue can be organized around week five for all the families, and could then be followed with a special presentation ceremony and speaker after the final week of the course.
- Keep each family on your database for future events and make certain that their son or daughter gets an early invitation to the following year's course.

ORGANIZING A GOLF DAY

Golf days are wonderful opportunities for the Christian golfer to enjoy the company of friends and colleagues and present them with the reality of the Christian message. Golf is such a popular sport and it is amazing how many folk have a set of clubs even if they don't play regularly.

A typical day's programme might be as follows:

9.30 a.m. – arrival and coffee
10.00 a.m. – morning competition
12.30 p.m. – soup and sandwiches
2.00 p.m. – afternoon competition
7.30 p.m. – evening meal, prize giving and guest speaker

Note: if you are planning a golf day for the first time, you may want to keep the day down to one round of golf plus the meal.

The above programme is based on a day consisting of twenty-seven holes of golf and, therefore, should be near to where most people live, and should not be a strenuous walk. It is probably only practical to organize a day like this during the week, as it may be virtually impossible to get on most golf courses for these times on a Saturday. Another disadvantage to organizing a golf day on a Saturday is that most courses are closed to visitors until late morning, which makes organizing anything more than eighteen holes difficult. Also, for family men and women it is not always a good idea to block off the whole of a Saturday for golf.

There are many advantages to holding the event during the week:

- It is easier to book a good golf course.
- If people book a day's holiday from work, there is less time pressure on them than at the weekend when domestic duties may call. In this regard, there will also be a greater take up to stay for the evening meal.
- Businessmen can take the opportunity to invite contacts.
- It is easier to book a good speaker.
- Most courses will be cheaper to play during the week than at the weekend.

Organizing the event locally also has advantages:

- Spouses can be invited to the evening meal and this tends to elevate the tone of the evening.
- The non-Christian target audience is, potentially, doubled.
- The likelihood of guests coming for the golf and then leaving before the meal is reduced.

For the afternoon competition, it is good to play the better golfers together. This means that the morning competition can enable hosts and guests to play together over nine holes. It is important, however, to decide on what sort of competition you want to play, and make sure you know the rules governing the competition. Confusion over who the eventual winners are can be a major irritant to your guests.

It is always difficult to select teams from individual applicants, so it is much better if people can be encouraged to get together a team of either two, three or four.

PLANNING

Find a golf course that will accept a block booking and make sure you negotiate a price than takes into account green fee, dinner, sandwich lunch (if required) and the use of a private room with a public address system. It is usual, but not necessary, to give all players a 'goody bag' (e.g. a couple of balls, tees and a chocolate bar) so this needs budgeting for as well.

Produce an invitation that makes it clear that the golf day includes the dinner. Do not accept entries from people who will not attend the dinner. The invitation should also make it clear that it is a church sports ministry event, since it is important that everyone knows what they are coming to. Specify the deadline for payment – last minute entries can easily confuse your planning. Ask if people have someone with whom they particularly want to play. Be sure that everyone knows when the day begins and enclose a map of how to find the course in a confirmation letter to all entrants.

The day needs to be billed as an outreach opportunity for bridge building and sharing the gospel

It is not always easy to get people to commit to a golf day, so you need to plan well in advance. Experience shows that it is less easy nowadays for people to get time off work than it was, a strong argument for making the event very attractive. Publicize the event regularly in your church bulletin and hand out flyers. If you can get twenty golfers and another ten or so guests for the evening meal, then you are well on track. Obviously, an entertaining speaker can add to the appeal and help with support. The day needs to be billed as an outreach opportunity for bridge building and sharing the gospel.

Finally, it may make sense to steer clear of a club that requires handicap certificates, since most golfers on an average church day will not be golf club members. All players, however, should be reminded of any dress code that may be in operation.

COST

For a midweek booking, you may be looking at any amount between £35 and £50. It would be more for a weekend. Green fees for a day could be £25 with coffee, soup and sandwiches, while the evening meal may vary between £10 and £15. On top of this, you need to consider your prize fund and the expenses for your guest speaker. Obviously, costs can be trimmed, usually by selecting carefully the course and facilities. A good marker for your eventual choice would be the opinion of the regular golfers in the church, since they are likely to be the core supporters of the event. Don't forget that you want an attractive venue for the evening meal.

On the question of cost, why not ask the church for some help towards the speaker's expenses and the give-away literature from Christians in Sport. Church members may also be happy to help towards a little bit of sponsorship for the prizes.

PRIZES

A quality first prize for the individual competition is a must, together with prizes for the winning team in the morning. For the afternoon competition it would be good to have prizes for the 1st, 2nd, and 3rd teams as well as one for the longest drive and nearest the pin. A hole in one would not be allowed to pass unnoticed either! Limit the prizes to one per person and have a few light-hearted ones thrown in: 'best effort', 'shot of the day' etc. With a bit of forward planning, it is amazing how you can gather prizes with a relatively modest budget.

ON ARRIVAL

A registration table should be set up in a convenient and obvious location. Each player should be given clear instructions for the day: tee off time, card showing the course layout, local rules and details of the format. The 'goody bag' provision will make a favourable impression. You might include a Christians in Sport tract on a well-known golfer.

Coffee should be available, and members of the organizing committee should welcome everyone and field any questions. Name badges for 'key' people would be useful.

THE PLAY

Ensure that a starter is present on the first tee. A shotgun format (where everyone starts at the same time, one group on the first tee, another on the second tee etc.) has the advantage of having everyone start and finish at the same time. If this format is used, then ensure that the gun is fired from somewhere it can be heard by everyone. This type of start usually means that the course has to be closed to the public, so you may have to resort to a two or three tee start.

Avoid slow play by urging players to 'pick-up' if they can no longer score on the hole. Ensure that at least one person on each team is an experienced golfer, familiar with both the rules and etiquette of the game. This person should be appointed the team captain so that his/her authority is unquestioned.

After the competition, check the cards as quickly as you can and then post the results on a board in the bar or foyer.

THE DINNER

It is always best to announce results and present prizes before the speeches. Sensitivity towards the audience should always be a priority, and the content of the gospel talk should be carefully considered. The majority of the players may be new to Christian things and would therefore profit more from the gentle testimony of a fellow golfer than a full gospel presentation. If, however, the company are used to sports ministry occasions, then a greater challenge may be called for, and with it the opportunity to invite Christ into their lives.

Sensitivity towards the audience should always be a priority

A second cup of coffee after the talk allows discussion of the day's activities and any points raised by the speaker. Return slips on the tables can be useful for gaining feedback and interest as well as advertising the next exploring Christianity course.

SOMETHING DIFFERENT

Philip Robson coordinates the golf ministry at Bethany Church, Houghton-le-Spring, in the north-east of England. Although golf days are a regular part of Bethany's calendar of events, Philip is keen to lay on something different from time to time. He has found that a trip to a local golf driving range for an evening can be great fun, especially for people who haven't played golf. The driving range will make clubs available if necessary, and might also provide their teaching professional for an hour or so in order to spend a few minutes with each group, going through the basics of the golf swing.

The party can then go back to church, or some suitable location, for a pizza and a speaker. The cost for such an evening can be quite reasonable and opens it up to a wider clientele. Such an occasion could also be useful for getting just the Christian golfers together and then 'selling' them the vision of a golf day.

FINAL NOTES

- A number of churches can come together for a golf day if any one church finds it difficult to go it alone.
- Prayer backing is essential for all aspects of the day, even the weather.
- A church golf day can be a stepping stone to the regional and national golf days organized by Christians in Sport.
- If the course is narrow, it would be good to have ball spotters at appropriate holes.
- Always be sure to make friends with the local pro and his/her assistant. Buying prizes from them will help a lot with relationships and co-operation.

The purpose of this chapter has been to give you a flavour of sports activities that some churches are doing very successfully. They are all very adaptable and can be tailored to suit your individual church situation and needs. It is important, however, that whatever you embark on you keep within the vision and mission statement of your ministry. This will always provide the backcloth to how you are progressing.

CHAPTER 6

Beacon Churches

You are the light of the world. A city on a hill cannot be hidden.
Matthew 5:14

For a number of years now, Christians in Sport has been working with churches, mainly through their local representatives. This has enabled a national network to be established and has played a part in developing sport and recreation ministry in many British churches. However, in January 2002 came the establishment of the 'beacon church' concept, with the selection of certain churches that were proving to be good role models for sports ministry. An initial wave of seven churches was soon to be joined by a further one before the summer of that year. The continuing vision is for the number of beacon churches to continue to grow, as good practice in sports ministry is replicated around the United Kingdom.

Beacon churches work with the following statement of purpose as common ground for their ministry:

> *'Sport and recreation ministry is not separate from the church and its other activities. It is an integral part of the total ministry of the church. The spiritual growth aspect makes it different from secular sport and recreation. It gives opportunities to share Christ with others who do not have a personal relationship with him, and will help develop spiritual growth in those already Christians.'*

Two verses from the Apostle Paul's first book to the church at Corinth remain key to this ministry: 'I have become all things to all men so that by all possible means I might save some' (1 Corinthians 9:22). 'So whether you eat or drink or whatever you do, do it all for the glory of God' (1 Corinthians 10:31).

A five-point plan provides an objective basis for beacon church development:

1. Provide for evangelistic opportunities.
2. Strengthen family life.
3. Influence the physical health of the individual.
4. Provide a setting for spiritual growth and development.
5. Plan an all year round programme to involve all ages from children to the active retired.

The following summaries give an insight into the work of beacon churches:

Bolton Pentecostal Church, Lancashire

The church has a small purpose-built sports hall that also doubles up as a children's crèche. Weekly aerobics classes ('Jump for Joy') take place here, with the specific intention of providing a service for friends and neighbours and bringing them into a Christian environment.

- Football figures prominently, and the church teams turn out regularly. Lifestyles and faith-sharing provide an outreach to the non-Christians in the teams. A squad from the church recently went to Italy to play and work alongside a missionary contact. There are regular football schools held during the summer, where Christian teaching and football skills operate alongside each other.

Lifestyles and faith-sharing provide an outreach to the non-Christians in the teams

- Regular rambles into the local countryside provide a contact with an area of the community not necessarily reached by aerobics and football.
- January 2002 saw the church take on a full-time staff member, Julian Wolstencroft, for youth and sports ministry.
- The church moved into top gear for the Commonwealth Games of 2002 held in Manchester. Ninety young people from one of Bolton's most deprived areas were transported into Manchester for four days of sporting and craft activities. At the final day's closing ceremony, thirty parents came to watch and, as well as being served refreshments, they were presented with a 'More Than Gold' Commonwealth Games pack. 50,000 people watched the mountain biking and cycling events, many of whom walked past the church's Commonwealth stall where they were able to receive refreshments, 'More Than Gold' booklets and copies of John's Gospel. BPC's canteen team also worked on this occasion with a drama team from Sydney and a choir from Uganda.

Diss Christian Community Church (DC3), Norfolk

This church has been operating with a full-time Director of Sport and Recreation for a number of years. In 1997, it built a sports hall extension to the nine-year-old church building, with its own kitchen, changing rooms and shower facilities. The sports hall is in use throughout the week with community access and, on Sundays, the removal of the separating partition allows the church to spill over into its arena.

- Children's football courses take place over a three-day period. As well as the coaching of basic skills, each day begins with a small cell group in which the ice-breaker may be something like 'What questions would you ask David Beckham if you had the chance to meet him?' This is then followed by a time of sharing joys or problems, learning a memory verse and then concluding with a prayer. Teenage helpers are involved with these groups and help them to consider standards of fair play, taking care of others, working as a team and many other life issues. The final day's presentation with parents in attendance always includes a gospel presentation from an adult footballer.
- 'Fun Fit' is a physical education skills class for 2–4 year olds. Parents are encouraged to work alongside their children and then help them practise at home. Refreshment breaks provide good contact opportunities and counselling help is provided in the case of personal difficulties.
- Three weekly keep fit classes are in operation: (1) Aerobics – the church sent one of its members on a

lengthy course to obtain the necessary qualification; (2) Power circuit training; (3) Gentle circuit training. From these have come one-to-one Bible study groups and an Alpha group from the aerobics class.

- The Badminton Club is made up of 70 per cent non-Christians and is seen as a fertile mission field. Friendly games are also played against other groups.
- The roller-skating club meets weekly, and from this the children can be directed to the church's Kids' Club and the schools' Christian unions.
- A men's football group uses the sports hall and is run by a member of the church.
- A short mat bowls club use the sports hall as a clubhouse. A couple from the church have become members and see this as their mission field.
- Sports breakfasts and dinners give opportunity for Christians to invite their friends to an outreach event. Personal invitations are also given to all adults who have used the sports hall during the year.
- In conjunction with the local Youth Service, a climbing wall has been installed in the sports hall and members of the church are being equipped to instruct in this area.

A forthcoming plan by the church is to organize training sessions for adults with learning disabilities wishing to train in preparation for the next Special Olympics.

Over 200 people who are not members of the church participate in centre activities each week

John Bussell is the Director of Sport and Recreation at DC3, as well as being the key contact person for Christians in Sport in East Anglia. In Stuart Weir's book *What the Book Says about Sport* John sums up DC3's vision for sports ministry:

> *'The purpose is to reach out into the community with the message of Jesus by providing a service to the community. Over 200 people who are not members of the church participate in centre activities each week and excellent contacts are being made.'*

First Presbyterian Church, Carrickfergus, Northern Ireland

The sport and recreation ministry at First Presbyterian started in 1998, after some of its members attended a Football World Cup roadshow run by Christians in Sport and held at the Crusaders Football Club in Belfast. One of these members, Ken Knocker, returned to Carrickfergus so inspired that he persuaded his minister to sanction the formation of the church's 'Fit for Life' department. Ken is the present director of the church's sports ministry.

First Presbyterian was operating as a resource church long before the establishment of the beacon church concept in January 2002 and has energized eight other churches in the town to be part of the ongoing sports ministry programme.

- Sixteen teams take part in the annual five-a-side football competition, when a Christian speaker gives the half-time pep talk.
- An inter-church 'It's a Knockout' draws around 300

folk as both spectators and participators. The evening opens with a brief, but challenging talk on the claims of Christ.

- First Presbyterian put on a go-karting event, together with other churches and their friends, having a gospel presentation as part of the session.
- Tenpin bowling, rambles and ladies hockey matches have all opened up opportunities to mix with the community at 'Fit for Life' events.
- Regular men's breakfast, attended by up to 180 people, enables active sporting Christians to share their faith.
- Sports services give opportunity for special invitations to go out to all the 'Fit for Life' contacts.
- The 'Fit for Life' team has taken a recent survey of church members' sporting interests in order to draw up fresh plans for the future.

Frinton Free Church, Frinton-on-Sea, Essex

Danny Lewis and his sports ministry team at Frinton have a very clear mission statement:

> *'To share the gospel with the local community through sport and recreation by resourcing and encouraging all sports ministry in the church.'*

They accomplish this in two key ways:

EVENTS

Between five and ten events are held every year, with each one appealing to all age groups. Each event aims at a particular group in the community. The 2002 programme included go-karting, tenpin bowling, archery, mixed netball, hockey, clay pigeon shooting, tennis tournament, golf day, walking afternoon, soccer coaching weekend, big screen football games and the 3rd Annual Schools' Football Tournament.

CLUBS

Frinton has a church football team, which is in a local church league that has been operating for about ten years.

There is also a badminton club, cricket club and aerobics class. The latter is run on church premises two to three times a week.

The church, which has a membership of over 500, provides a budget, and prayer support during the events

There are specific roles for the sports ministry team of seven. These include areas like events, promotion and follow-up. The church, which has a membership of over 500, provides a budget, and prayer support during the events.

Glenwood Church, Cardiff, South Wales

The Director of Sports Ministry, Ian Sutton, has been on a number of Ambassadors in Sport football tours and uses his considerable experience in this area to run a football academy at the church. Each week he works with 12–15 year olds from the local estate: youngsters who would not normally be found within touching distance of the church. Friendly matches are arranged periodically, and four of the boys attended Christians in Sport's Brecon Camp with Ian.

- Football schools are also a feature of the year's programme. Ninety youngsters between the ages of seven and fourteen attend each school and, during the week, Christian teaching figures prominently.
- Howard Dobson, active in sports ministry for many years, runs a weekly men's keep fit class. This caters for a wide range of people and is a good contact with young men from the nearby estate.
- The cricket team has a good number of fixtures every summer and Glenwood takes it upon itself to organize a church seven-a-side tournament for Cardiff churches.
- During the summer months, the church encourages many of the young people it has contact with to attend Christians in Sport camps, as well as providing a good number of quality leaders and coaches at the same time.
- The 2002 Football World Cup saw Glenwood run big screen viewings for friends and families. The combination of a great lunch and exciting atmosphere provided a fine basis for friendship evangelism.
- Boxing Day morning has a long tradition of playing the Glenwood football match on the local park. It provides a great opportunity to mix and share with visiting relatives and family members who don't make church regularly.

Opportunity to mix and share with visiting relatives and family members who don't make church regularly

St Jude's Church, Southsea, Hampshire

Chris Cox heads up a very active programme at St Jude's. He prayed, not too long ago, for another Christian rugby player to join the church. Within a year, three had arrived, and all four ended up playing for Portsmouth!

- Badminton, table tennis and football tournaments are held during the year, as is a swimming gala for the church and their friends. Splash time allows parents to be with their young children and for relationships to be forged with non-church folk.
- The five-a-side football team plays weekly in a secular league and has progressed from being bottom of the league to the 'fair play' trophy winners and league runners up. On alternate Fridays, there is non-competitive football for local churches at a nearby school. The teams are a mixture of Christians and non-Christians.

The football team has visited Druisburg in Germany for two successive years

- The football team has visited Druisburg in Germany for two successive years in order to play in a charity tournament and raise money for children with AIDS. As well as having a great time, the team enjoyed the opportunity for fellowship and faith-sharing.
- The church has a qualified instructor to run the weekly keep fit class.
- Ladies of all ages meet alternate Fridays at a local school to play netball.

- Between February and May touch rugby is a feature of the programme. Ages range from 12 to 50 and include both sexes.
- Cricket matches run throughout the season against local teams and provide another opportunity to invite folk to the end of season sports breakfast.
- A supposedly 'one-off' Saturday sports morning for the under 10s proved to be so successful that plans are in hand to run it on a regular basis.
- A sports award breakfast is held every June to recognize all the effort and achievement over the year. There is a guest speaker to present the awards and bring a challenge from the world of faith and sport.

Molesey Community Church, West Molesey, Surrey

The vision of Mark Blythe and his team is to be a resource church for sports ministry reaching out locally, nationally and internationally.

- Four adult teams play in local secular and church leagues. Teams enter the national CPO (Christian Publicity Organization) Cup.
- 'Moves Fitness' is a weekly aerobics dance session and is led by church members in a local school hall. It is very popular and has led to invitations to the church ladies' monthly meal evenings.
- There is a monthly men's curry night for all those playing in the various teams – a great opportunity for friendship building.

- An outreach golf day takes place every year.
- Tenpin bowling evenings for the football club players and their partners give the Christian members of the team real opportunities for faith-sharing.
- The annual awards night for the football club attracts around ninety players and their partners. The evening is comprised of video footage, testimony and prizes, while the season's report in printed colour includes several testimonies and is distributed at the end of the evening.
- A go-karting day with Discovery Ministries is a popular event. A meal and a gospel presentation follows the day's karting.
- Saturday morning football clinics for the 5–14 age group.
- A coffee shop with a large TV screen provides a clean language, non-smoking, child-friendly atmosphere for significant England and other big games.
- Cricket matches are arranged against local club, pub and police. Games start with open prayer.
- Five-mile fun run for football club players and others interested.

MCC seeks to be a resource to the nation by administering the National Christian Cricket Cup

- MCC seeks to be a resource to the nation by administering the National Christian Cricket Cup and the National Christian Golf Cup as well as releasing Mark to organize the National Football Festival.

- Stages an annual high profile celebrity football match against ex-professionals from Chelsea, Spurs etc, thereby raising money for local charities and raising the awareness of the church in the community.

The aim of all the activities is to develop friendships, with a view to sharing the gospel at the appropriate time. A number of opportunities arise where clear gospel presentations can feature. Some activities deliberately include spouses and partners in order to strengthen family life and widen the contact base.

St Francis C of E, Guildford, Surrey

As well as being the team rector and director of sports ministry at St Francis, the Reverend Clive Potter is also the Guildford Diocesan Advisor on sports ministry and the recently appointed Chaplain to Surrey Football Association. Under his leadership, there are around 800 young people taking part in church-run Saturday football clubs. His position also enables him to carry out speaking engagements at sports dinners and on radio programmes. His good contacts with Wimbledon Football Club, Fulham Football Club, the Football Association and the British Sports Trust all give him tremendous opportunity for faith-sharing.

There are around 800 young people taking part in church-run Saturday football clubs

- Football kits are sent to Sierra Leone and, through this, the church is able to develop its own mission link with that country.

- St Francis Sports is an approved mini football centre and offers weekly coaching for 6–12 year olds.
- Football and cross-country coaching sessions are held in various schools.
- An annual charity football tournament supports the 'Neighbours in Need' campaign and strengthens community links.
- Clive is aware of the need to train people up as community sports leaders, and gives a lot of his time to equipping others in CSLA and FA awards. See below for further information on both of these.

These eight beacon churches are examples of what is beginning to take place all over the United Kingdom. The prayer of Christians in Sport is that such churches will start a fire that cannot be put out and one that will provide a glow that is attractive to all and life changing to many.

Equipping the Church's Sports Department

Any church that is serious about its sport and recreation ministry would do well to encourage its members to go on courses for sports qualifications. Here are just a few that could prove to be significant:

1. COMMUNITY SPORTS LEADER AWARD (CSLA)

Since 2001, Christians in Sport have trained a group of sixth formers at their summer camps, through this award that has been developed by the British Sports Trust (BST). It has proved to be a superb way of developing young leaders' skills, through the practical aspects of sport. The BST states: 'The huge popularity of sport makes it the ideal medium for the training and development of young people. The skills which a candidate develops throughout the course assist him/her in organizing sport or recreation for other people and help to develop vital life skills such as managing oneself and others, teamwork and communication.'

The CSLA, delivered during the Christians in Sport camps, has revealed a remarkable increase in confidence and self-esteem in the candidates, while the practical experience gained provides lifelong skills in self-management and leadership. This nationally recognized award is a great opportunity for the church to train sports leaders through their own qualified tutor. The link with the community in sports provision would be enormously advanced by this initiative.

This nationally recognized award is a great opportunity for the church to train sports leaders

COURSE CONTENT

The CSLA gives people aged 16 and over the skills needed to lead groups in safe sporting and recreational activity. The majority of the course is practical in nature, with an emphasis on learning through doing, rather than through written work. There are eight units to the award:

1. Organizational skills
2. Safety in sport
3. Know your friends
4. Fitness sessions for sport
5. Organization of events and competitions
6. Improvisation and adapted games
7. Games and activity experience
8. Ten hours voluntary leadership experience

All units must be satisfactorily completed.

DURATION OF THE COURSE

Factors such as the student/teacher ratio, the number and experience of the group and the number and experience of the tutors, all influence the overall length of the course. However, an average course involves twenty-five to thirty hours of tutored time, excluding the ten hours of voluntary leadership experience.

COSTS

There is no charge for registering for a Community Sports Leader Award, but tutors must purchase a Tutor Resource Pack. There is also a charge per candidate and, in return, each candidate will receive a Community Sports Leader Award logbook, certificate on completion and one year's liability insurance. Each candidate will receive a certificate and badge on successful completion of the course.

BRITISH SPORTS TRUST

This is a registered charity (no. 299810) that runs three other awards as well as the CSLA. These are:

- *Junior Sports Leader*
- *Higher Sports Leader*
- *Basic Expedition Leader*

Further information on all these awards can be found (at the time of writing) on the web site – www.bst.org.uk

2. LEVEL 1 CERTIFICATE IN COACHING FOOTBALL (THE FOOTBALL ASSOCIATION)

Many churches have football teams, and youngsters of all ages are crying out to be coached in this most popular of sports. The local church would be taking a huge step forward in its sports ministry development by arranging for one or more of its members to gain this qualification.

Youngsters of all ages are crying out to be coached in this most popular of sports

The Level 1 Certificate in Coaching Football (L1CCF) is awarded in partnership with the Football Association and is one of a number of coaching qualifications awarded by 1st 4sport Qualifications.

The Level 1 vocationally related qualification provides the potential coach with the opportunity to study and be assessed for both practical and theoretical aspects of coaching football at this level.

He or she can then coach grassroots church and club teams for children and young people aged 7–16 years. The qualification is delivered through approved centres, many of which will be FA County Football Associations and can be studied on a part-time or full-time basis.

Qualification structure

Three units of study comprise this qualification:

1. *Safe and ethical football*
2. *Football basics*
3. *Delivering football coaching sessions for young people*

All three units must be completed to receive the L1CCF. The structured delivery and assessment programme lasts between twenty-four and forty hours, and is likely to be spread over a number of days or weekends.

Qualification objectives

The qualified coach will be able to:

- demonstrate an ability to safely organize and supervise football activities including mini soccer, small sided and conditioned games
- promote and establish working relationships and high standards of behaviour with players, coaches, parents and officials in the overall development of association football
- demonstrate an understanding of related aspects of coaching children in football and identify and adapt football activities and sessions for a variety of different age groups

Further information

For more details on Football Association courses and other sports qualifications look on the following web sites:

www.TheFA.com
www.1st4sportqualifications.com

3. SPORTS LEADERSHIP AND INTERCULTURAL STUDIES (SLICS)

From 1999 to 2002, Christians in Sport pioneered the first British and European year-long sports ministry qualification under the direction of Graham Daniels. It was based on one day a week of lectures in Bible overview, leadership skills and evangelism tools, with the rest of the week spent with the students involved in schools and church work. Over that period of time, thirty-four postgraduates were equipped as potential sports ministers in many different aspects of church life.

Thirty-four postgraduates were equipped as potential sports ministers in many different aspects of church life

This Academy Course, which was based in Cambridge, has now been superseded by a one year certificate in Higher Education in Sports Leadership and Intercultural studies at All Nations Christian College, Ware, Hertfordshire.

The SLICS programme is a thirty-week residential course, leading to the award of a Certificate in Higher Education validated by the Open University, the Higher Sports Leaders Award (awarded by the British Sports Trust), National Governing Body coaching, officiating awards of the student's choice and a first aid qualification. The practical elements of the course will also include event organization and working with a range of community groups including primary school children, disabled people and older people.

The course consists of twelve modules in four fields:

1. **Personal**
   Personal development and practical ministry.

2. **Biblical**
   Introduction to the Hebrew Bible.
   Introduction to the New Testament.

3. **Intercultural**
   Social anthropology.
   Choice of the following depending on timetable availability
   (i) History of Christian mission
   (ii) Church planting

4. **Sports Leadership**
   Theology and ethics of competition
   The global development of Christian mission
   Integrating sportspeople into the Christian community
   Sports leadership and management
   Higher Sports Leader Award

4. SPORTS LEADERSHIP SHORT COURSE

This course of nine days duration is geared to those who are unable to commit to a full-time course for a full year. It will be helpful for church workers, summer camp volunteers and leaders of university and players' groups as well as those wishing to go on short-term sports missions in the summer vacation. As well as introductory lectures in sports ministry, the Community Sports Leader Award (CSLA) will also be included.

Further details of both these courses can be obtained from:

All Nations Christian College
Easneye
Ware
Hertfordshire, SG12 8LX
Tel: +44 (0)1920 461243
Email: sportsleadership@allnations.ac.uk

It is hoped that such courses will be the beginning of an array of courses on offer (degrees, masters etc) to those who feel the call of God on their lives for ministry in the world of sport and recreation. The author of this book wouldn't want the twenty-first century to be too old before the British Church saw both the importance and the necessity for appointing full-time sports ministers. Train the best to be the best, is a motto close to the heart of God and one that should motivate all disciples of Christ.

CHAPTER 7

The Next Generation

Reputation is what you bring with you. Character is what you can take away.
Herbert Spencer

The world has never been any different. It longs for heroes that it can enjoy, emulate and sometimes even worship. Unfortunately, too many heroes are taken in by their own publicity and woefully fall short of the intended target. The talented musician who is an inspiration to many, finds the world of drugs and compromising relationships all too attractive to resist. The footballer whose shirt and number adorns the back of young and old alike, can't avoid using the field of play for aggressive and vengeful behaviour. Sadly, these gifted people are role models to a younger generation that can't always discern the difference between reputation and character. It is here where the Christian athlete can take over the scoring. To reflect the life of Christ in the world of sport is both challenging and daunting. However, there can be no finer thing than a person living for Jesus in the intense laboratory of the sporting world.

There are three areas in particular where Christians in Sport has sought to provide an atmosphere where young people can be encouraged in Christian living and observe those who are role modelling the gospel in the world of sport.

1. SPORTS CAMPS

For nearly a decade now, Christians in Sport has run summer camps for teenagers who are passionate about their sport. Coaching at these camps is of the highest level in the major sports of football, tennis, hockey, rugby, netball, athletics, basketball and golf and is delivered during intense morning and afternoon sessions. An early morning run around the campuses of Christ College, Brecon and Repton School in Derbyshire, together with daily Team Challenge activities, serve to supplement all the coaching going on. The leadership team of coaches, team leaders, speakers and support staff is always a large one so that a ratio of two leaders to every three athletes can be maintained. The purpose of the camp is to demonstrate the Christian life in the world of sport, so that the young athletes can be challenged to walk that way themselves. For Christian youngsters, the camp is a time of growth and fresh challenges, while for others it is often the very start of their spiritual journey with Jesus.

The purpose of the camp is to demonstrate the Christian life in the world of sport

Talented young men and women in their late teens and early twenties provide role model examples during the week in a variety of ways:

- The early morning run sees a full camp turn out (250–300) with the team leaders and coaches running alongside the athletes.
- A quality cool down and stretching session is followed by a five-minute testimony from one of the leaders.

- The after breakfast team meeting is an exciting mixture of sports video footage, lively worship songs, pulsating quizzes, interviews and brief but interesting talks: all of which communicate to the athletes the challenging adventure of being a Christian.

- The morning coaching sessions work the athletes hard and always include a devotional break in the middle. This provides a sports value moment for the coach who may choose to look from a Christian perspective at such areas as teamwork, leadership, winning with humility, losing with dignity, and persistence. The athletes themselves will also be given an opportunity to share how God is working in their lives. The afternoon coaching sessions would follow on similar lines.

- The daily Team Challenge competition gives the leaders many opportunities to stress and develop Christian character in their respective teams. Seven-minute games of halo, kwik cricket, ultimate Frisbee and football contribute to a junior and senior league, and help to bind both team and leaders together. The leaders don't take part in these games, but spend all their time on the touchline encouraging and supporting their charges. All games are concluded with both teams forming a huddle for a prayer together. Prayers every seven minutes on the sports field . . . now there's a revolutionary concept!

Prayers every seven minutes on the sports field . . . now there's a revolutionary concept!

- Free time before the evening meal often finds the athletes and leaders trying their hand at different sports and developing friendships.

- The evening meeting is a magazine style programme aimed right at the heart of youth sports culture with state of the art technology. Loud music, sporting clips from well-known films, on-stage challenges and competitions, and thought-provoking talks. This is followed by a time in dormitories for all athletes and their leaders in order to study the Bible and discuss the theme of the day, as well as the major point from the evening talk. These times have seen many young athletes give their lives to Christ over the years.
- During the dormitory times, the coaches gather to have their own time together. As well as sharing their experiences of the day, they also pray for the many teams as they meet to discuss the claims of Christ on their lives. The desire of the coaches is not merely to be Christian coaches, but to learn together how they might coach 'Christianly'.

By the end of camp, the athletes are beginning to see how the secular and the spiritual life can be as one in the world of sport. The coaches and leaders they have come to admire are constantly at pains to demonstrate the discipline of following Jesus as well as obeying the rules of their sport. Respecting your opponent, showing integrity in your relationship with your team-mates, having the right attitude to match officials, and coping with a poor performance are all key issues that are more easily appreciated and understood when they come from an experienced coach.

Team leaders continue their contact with the athletes throughout the year with regular correspondence, as they encourage them to keep on keeping on in the Christian life and in their sporting development.

A similar sports camp or sports week could be put into operation by a church or group of churches. Glenwood Church in Cardiff, one of Christians in Sport's beacon churches, runs a football week with youngsters from their local estate, seeking to integrate them into the life of the church at the same time. Several of these boys have also attended the national camp at Brecon.

Sport is the language that plugs generation gaps and opens up communication channels

Sport is the language that plugs generation gaps and opens up communication channels. The coming together of generations in a sports camp setting only bears out the remarkable nature of this medium. It is fertile ground for the things of God to be demonstrated and embraced so that, as each new generation comes through, there will always be a good crop of those who love their Lord and love their sport.

2. NIGHT OF CHAMPIONS

A decade ago, an ex Chicago Bears and LA Rams footballer called Steve Connor introduced the concept of Night of Champions to Christians in Sport. He had run this event in the United States while working for the Fellowship of Christian Athletes (FCA), and began with only a handful of people. In 1996, he was invited back to the States as the keynote speaker at a Night of Champions in Los Angeles and spoke in front of 6,000 young people in the football stadium. Such a development in a short period of time indicates the potential to be found in this sporting event that challenges young people both physically and spiritually. It is well within the compass of the local church to organize a Night of Champions, providing it does its praying, planning and preparation well. Christians in Sport has run the event at several locations around the country and introduced it as a 'More Than Gold' event for the Commonwealth Games in Manchester 2002. The following salient points are extracted from a manual produced by the Christians in Sport Youth Department.

INTRODUCTION

Night of Champions is an evening for sporty youngsters to enjoy, play and compete in various sports, and an opportunity to give them an insight into the Christian faith. The local church has thousands of young people in its area with a passion for sport, and the medium of Night of Champions will enable it to reach, teach, nurture and sustain them in the gospel.

The local church has thousands of young people in its area with a passion for sport

The vision of this event is to make a difference for Christ in the sub-culture of sport and to equip the local church in this area. Night of Champions doesn't have all the answers, but goes some way towards challenging young people, in the area where they enjoy being, with the life-changing message of Jesus. It is suggested that the details are adapted as necessary since no two churches or their communities are the same.

BACKGROUND

Night of Champions was first introduced into the UK in 1996 around the European Football Championships. In Leeds and Liverpool, in particular, youth groups in the region would bring teams to compete in a multi-sports tournament and hear the good news of Jesus in a multi-media presentation. Over 800 youngsters turned up at these two venues and the evenings were heralded a great success.

A little later, in 1999, the Christians in Sport Academy began to regularly facilitate this event and made many links with church youth groups and local secondary schools. It proved to be a fantastic way for building relationships at the foundational level. The concern at the time, however, was that it was merely a stab in the dark into a culture and community where sport can have so much impact as a catalyst in bringing Jesus Christ to young people. For this reason it was decided that Night of Champions could be used for two separate outcomes:

1. *Unity amongst communities/towns, as established youth groups are invited to bring their sporty youngsters to participate in an evening of sport and a chance to hear the good news of Jesus.*
2. *As part of a church-based outreach strategy in an attempt to empower their young members to go into their own schools and invite their friends to a credible, non-cringy, Christian event where the sport is the attraction.*

If the second option is pursued, the church needs to make sure that there is an ongoing outreach strategy, so that youngsters who come to Night of Champions and are interested in the Christian faith can be slotted into the reaching-teaching-nurturing-sustaining process. The idea of sport must never be dropped throughout this process and must be included in the different stages of discipleship.

ON THE NIGHT OUTLINE

This can be adapted according to local conditions. In the winter and spring terms, Night of Champions is very much an 'in house' event and will generally last for a couple of hours. Many favour a Friday/weekend evening and the following outline is a typical example of one of these.

6.30 p.m.	Registration and warm-up games
7.00 p.m.	Welcome and introduction to the event
7.10 p.m.	Competition begins
8.40 p.m.	Gospel presentation
8.55 p.m.	Results and presentations
9.00 p.m.	Home

The talk/gospel presentation needs to be relevant, real and appropriate to the situation

In the summer the event could, weather permitting, be held outside. These events will generally be longer and may include a barbecue and big screen sporting event, e.g. World Cup.

The talk/gospel presentation needs to be relevant, real and appropriate to the situation. Visuals are fantastic when linked with a sporty theme through video footage and testimony.

THE GAMES

It is important that all the rules of the games you are playing are explained fully to all teams at the beginning of the night. This will save a good deal of time as teams turn up to play the games.

- **Football**

  Five-a-side basic football rules: no offside, area restrictions apply, rolling substitutes. Under arm roll-ons replace throw-ins and the goalkeeper must roll it out.

- **Unihoc**

  Five-a-side, basic hockey rules: no offside, no area restrictions, rolling substitutes. No deliberate kicking of the puck (be lenient with accidental feet), goalies can kick the puck but only in the goal area. No slashing with the sticks, and be aware of any deliberate dangerous play.

- **Basketball**

  Five-a-side, basic basketball rules: no double dribble, no travelling, minimal contact (please be strict so things don't get out of hand). Be liberal with the three seconds rule in the key and the giving of free shots if fouled in the act of shooting.

- **Alternative Netball**

  Five-a-side, basic netball rules: no footwork (this will be hard, but just stop them moving with the ball), minimal contact, players must be a metre away to mark, three seconds with the ball.

  Special rules: the game is played with one post in half a court. Once the attack is broken up, the intercepting team must pass the ball beyond the half way line before beginning their attack.

- **Volleyball**

  Five-a-side. You can have rolling subs. Serve behind the back line, rotate the team to serve. Up to three touches on each side before it has to go over; a player can't have two consecutive touches. No let serves: if the ball hits the net on a serve the serve is handed over. You can only win points on your serve. Keep scoring until the time is up.

- **Ultimate Frisbee**

Five-a-side. A point is scored when the Frisbee is caught in the end zone. No running with the Frisbee and minimal contact. When the Frisbee hits the ground, it will go to the opposing team from the one that last contacted it. After a point is scored the opposing team will start with the Frisbee from the end zone they are defending. (Note: if you are playing outside and it is windy, you should have a half time and change ends to ensure no disadvantage to either team.)

- **Halo**

Five-a-side. Very similar to bench ball but the target person holds an up-turned hockey stick while standing inside a large hoop. A point is scored when the target person catches the quoit on the stick while still inside the goal circle (hoop). No running with the quoit in hand; if the quoit hits the floor, the play goes to the other team. No pulling of the quoit off the stick. If two players catch the quoit at the same time, there is a throw up. The target person can be changed at any time during the game.

- **Kwik Cricket**

Both teams will bat and field for a certain length of time. The referee will bowl. One run is scored each time you run to a cone (cones are about five strides away left and right of the stumps). You must run whether you hit the ball or not. The bowler can bowl as soon as the ball is in his hands, whether the batter is there or not. You can be out by being bowled, caught or hitting your wicket. There is no lbw (leg before wicket).

- **Table Tennis**

Doubles. Pairs must hit the ball in turn. Play to nine points, two serves and then change. If a serve hits the net then it is a let. Teams can score a point whether it was their serve or not. Play as many games as possible. Pairs can be changed in between games. Whichever team wins the most games is the victor.

- **Badminton**

All the players from the teams can play this. Each person takes it in turn to hit the shuttle and then runs to the back of the queue of their team. If they miss the shuttle or hit it out, they sit out (make sure they sit in a safe place). When the last player from either team is out, the rest of that team can join again. *Count the number of people who are knocked out in each team!* The team which has the fewest knocked out is the winner.

- **Netball Shooting**

As many players as possible, but make sure each team has the same number of players. Each team has a ball. Mark a spot on the floor and stand the first person on it, with the rest of the team lining up behind. Give the ball to the last person in the line whose job it is to hand the ball over the head of the person in front.

This person then passes the ball through the legs of the person in front and so on until the ball reaches the first person. This person then shoots for the net and collects their own shot before running to the back of the line with the ball to start the process again. Score two points for a goal and one if the ring is hit.

INSTRUCTIONS FOR REFEREES

It is important that the evening's games are played in a competitive manner, but also that fair play and fun are seen as being key to its eventual success. It is good for referees to have clear direction on their responsibilities:

1. Check the teams as they arrive and ensure they are entered on the scorecard correctly (check the running order if you are unsure). It is vital to have the right teams on the card.
2. Start and finish on the whistle. The event is centrally timed in different venues and *timing is crucial*. If the teams are not there at the start, then a shorter game has to be played – this is the same for stoppages during the game e.g. injuries. The games can't overrun.
3. Try to be firm in enforcing the rules. If you are lenient early, the teams will take advantage, but if you explain the rules and then stick firmly to them, the games will be easier to manage. Please be especially strict on deliberate foul play and ensure that the team leader is aware of any problems you have with the players so they can calm them down and have a word with them where necessary.
4. We are trying to encourage sportsmanship and fair play, so please praise it when it occurs. As a

visible sign to promoting this, encourage the teams to shake hands after every event. You may need to instigate this and help it stay in the spirit it was intended.

5. Somebody will be appointed to collect the scorecards following each round of matches. Please make it clear who won and what the final score was.

INSTRUCTIONS FOR TEAM LEADERS

Welcome to the Night of Champions. The aim of the evening is for sporty young people to enjoy, play and compete in sport and to give them a brief presentation on an aspect of sport and Christianity.

For the event to run smoothly your help is vital!

1. You will have a running order with your team's fixtures highlighted. Timing is very tight with a three-minute change-over between matches. The timing will roll on, so get to the next match quickly, since the referee will not wait.
2. As we are aiming for good sportsmanship, please encourage your team to shake hands after each game. Do this quickly and in the spirit it is intended.
3. The referee's decision is final and it is important that you accept this. You are setting an example to your team and they will look to you for a lead. We want the young people to have fun and approach the games with a positive attitude.

SCORING

5 points for a win
3 points for a score draw
2 points for a no score draw
1 point for a loss

In the event of a draw at the end of the evening, the team with the most goals scored will be the winners. If it is still a draw then goal difference will be taken into account.

3. GAME OF TWO HALVES (GO2H)

The Tearfund Youth Team in association with Viz a Viz and Christians in Sport launched GO2H in 1998. Its aim is to raise money by playing sport of all descriptions and at the same time raise awareness of the issues facing communities in the developing world.

It provides churches, and young people in particular, with the opportunity to enjoy their sport but also to make a difference in lands of deprivation and suffering.

Christians in Sport took over ownership of GO2H in April 2002 and opened up the project to all individuals and churches in their sports ministry network. As a sports project for sports people, GO2H is unique as a mission initiative, with the added advantage of involving and encouraging many people at home as well as abroad. Friends who are not yet Christians will get involved with GO2H because they want to support overseas projects and play their part. The main difference with these projects is that they are run by Christians who desire to share the love of Jesus with those they serve.

KENYA

In Spring 2002, a group of eleven young people representing Christians in Sport visited Kenya on a trip organized by the Tearfund Transform Team. The objective was to visit the site of a number of GO2H projects in Nairobi and be of service to the Kenyans involved in these initiatives. Football is the great attraction for young people in this part of the world, and before the young people arrived, equipment and finances had already got the projects off to a good start. There is a particular need in Nairobi, where many children, attracted to the city for work, end up abused and homeless or living in slum areas. Football competitions and clinics offer the greatest opportunity to reach out to these youngsters with the love of Jesus.

The two-week trip served to transform the lives of the young people in the party as they saw the difference GO2H was making. They were able to take £1,200 of sports equipment with them on the flight and experienced first-hand the overwhelming delight of the recipients. Involvement in coaching clinics and relationships formed with the Kenyan young people enabled the British youngsters to share their giftings.

GREAT IDEAS

There have been many creative activities run around the country on behalf of GO2H.

- Leamington Spa Baptist Church sponsored one of their young athletes, Jenny Christie, for every race she won and every personal best she attained. Jenny had a good summer, with wins in the All England Championships and at international level also. This particular project scored on two fronts. The church began to encourage her talent and pray for her when she was competing. Jenny felt supported and had even more motivation to perform well because GO2H benefited. It was good sport psychology!

- One group had a twenty-four-hour Sportathon! A wide range of people were encouraged to take part in aerobics, a sunrise cycle ride or the swimming of lengths at the local pool. Then there was an evening sports quiz to round the day off.
- Christians in Sport personnel promised to have their hair bleached if the athletes and leaders on the Repton Sports Camp could raise £500 for GO2H. When a target of £1,500 was reached, the General Director of Christians in Sport appeared to have formed his own colourful boy band by the next morning! Not to be outdone, the athletes and leaders on the Brecon Sports Camp pledged £800 for the Dean of the Camp to complete the Great North Run.

A HELPFUL LIST

GO2H can be a great opportunity to make contact with your community in an extremely worthwhile venture that benefits others and proclaims Christ. Here are some activities that will hopefully be an inspiration to some of the readers of this book:

- Seek sponsorship at the start of your sports season – number of goals scored, clean sheets for goalkeepers, wickets taken, runs made etc. This is a great motivation to have a good season.
- Tennis tournaments with pay to play emphasis.
- Triathlons, marathons, Three Peaks Challenge.
- Games afternoons – pay to compete or be sponsored for scoring.

- Table football fun and games evenings.
- Sports auctions.
- Sports wear day – wear your kit for church and pay for the privilege.
- Cycle/rowing machine challenge with as many people going the distance as possible.
- All night indoor competition – volleyball, basketball, five-a-side football – sponsorship by the hour and/or for points/goals scored.

The possibilities are endless, but the sports emphasis enables people who speak the language of sport to make a difference in a world crying out for love and care.

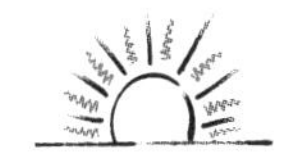

CHAPTER 8

The Second Half

You do not stop playing when you grow old; you grow old when you stop playing. Anon

When churches are first approached about sport and recreation ministry, their thoughts are usually centred on either the young people's work or the possibility of a church football team. The prospect of an all year round programme with adults is generally far from their minds, with little or no consideration given to those in the second half of their lives. It is, in fact, this group of senior adults, sometimes called the active retired, who are anxious to keep up their fitness levels and are on the lookout for new challenges in their lives. The market place has recognized the buying power of this ever-increasing group of people but, as yet, the church does not seem to have appreciated the influence they can have for the Kingdom of God.

The Office for National Statistics produced the 2002 Census, which revealed that the United Kingdom had more people over the age of 60 than under the age of 16, and that one million of its fifty eight million inhabitants were over 85! By 2020, one third of the population in the UK will be over

50, with the majority expected to live for a further two or three decades after passing the big five-O. If the first twenty-five years of our lives can be described as 'preparation' and the next twenty-five as 'occupation' then there is no reason why the 50 to 75 years bracket can't be seen as 'transformation'. Unmissable Ltd, a company that has set out to offer its clients the chance to make their dreams come true, carried out a survey of a representative sample of 500 people in Britain. The survey discovered that the ages at which people make lists of the things they dream of doing in their lives proved to be the very young and the seriously mature. As people grew up, the survey results concluded, the wish list went away, but as the second half of life arrived, it was revised, updated and finally used as an agenda for the rest of life.

Boomer Generation

This boomer senior adult group that is now in the ascendant, grew up in a world of leisure, whereas their parents led harder lives which were work orientated throughout. The younger group views leisure as an expectation, not a reward. They have more time to plan for early retirement by saying 'What will I do?' rather than seeing it as a date to aim for and then giving everything up. Time and money will be spent on quality things and experiences.

However, this boomer generation is also an unseeded generation. Largely, they have not been brought up on Christian principles and don't know their Bible. Their desires lie in a number of directions:

- They are looking for a variety of experiences.
- They want to feel that they are being useful.

- They want to try new things.
- They are seeking a younger self-image.
- They like the personal touch in services and comfortable surroundings.
- They are planning for an expanded health span rather than merely a life span. Lifestyle and medical care serve to help this along.

Growing Old Slowly

Dr Ken Cooper's philosophy is that 'it is better to grow old than to get old'. Ageing is inevitable, but it is not inevitable that we do it at an accelerated rate. Average life expectancy in the UK now exceeds 75, yet many who come into that category are not really living, they are often just existing. Chronic health conditions have deprived them of their independence and self-control. A study on independence and ageing published in the US Public Health Services Prevention Report in October 1991 served to illustrate the enormity of this problem. The investigation revealed that in 1980, when life expectancy in the United States was nearly 74 years of age, the expectancy for a healthy life was only 62 years. In other words, Americans lived nearly twelve years of their life expectancy with some sort of chronic condition e.g. heart problem, joint disease or back ailment. These conditions were seriously affecting their quality of life. Cooper, in his book *Faith-Based Fitness,* goes on to surmise: 'But such a depressing result isn't inevitable. Our goal as we grow older should be, as

'It is better to grow old than to get old'

gerontologists say, "to square off the curve". What this means is that as you age, bodily functions can be plotted on a linear graph with the curve dipping downwards from maximum health and capacity in the younger years to a cessation of functioning at death. For most people, there is a steady decline in physical functioning – a gradual dipping curve on the graph – which in effect leads to slow death in the last twelve years of life. But those who enter the advanced years in a healthy, fit state can actually condense the time of senility or limited capacity to function into a short period immediately prior to death.'

Benefits of Fitness

There can be no doubt that fitness for those over 50 can have enormous benefits:

- A greater sense of fulfilment and well-being.
- Improved energy levels.
- Ability to focus on family activity and togetherness.
- Being a more active parent and grandparent.
- Less time spent in the doctor's surgery or the hospital ward.
- Freedom to help your relatives with their lives rather than them worrying about you.

Unfortunately, for many the picture is quite different. They are overweight, bulky around the middle and wouldn't contemplate breaking into a short run to save their lives. Any extended physical activity only aggravates muscles that have long been dormant and leg muscles quickly start to cramp when there is a need to hurry for a late appointment.

The gap between wishing you were fit and getting fit seems insurmountable to so many. What they need is a ready-made programme that will cater for both their physical and their spiritual needs.

Where the Church Comes In

We must first face the fact that this 'second half' age group is one for which the church, so far, has no developed strategy. It is a group with high expectations, looking for changes in lifestyle and carrying a lot of experience. The local church will inevitably have such a group within its walls and an even larger group outside. In meeting the leisure and recreational needs of this group, the church will impact its community for Christ in a big way.

The New Breed

For those in the second half of life, new titles are often being bandied about. 'Grey power' came to the fore in 2002, when several football managers in their sixties found themselves in charge of successful Premier League clubs. Not for them a quiet desk job away from all the action. 'Senior powerhouses' are those who manage to retain the power of youth into their old age – they box below their chronological age. In recent years, Everett Hosack picked up gold medals in the 60 metres, 200 metres, the shot, throwing the weight and

'Senior powerhouses' box below their chronological age

the superweight in the United States Masters Indoor Championships at Boston. He was 98, and competes for the Over the Hill Track Club! Hosack had retired from competitive sports in the 1920s, but took it up again when he was 77. When asked if his daily garlic and multivitamin pills were the secret to long life, he replied that it was too early to tell because he had only been taking them since he was 95!

Harry Meistrup from Denmark is the world's oldest tennis player at 101. He plays each week against his 87-year-old wife for two hours with no rest in between games. Noel Johnson from San Diego, took up sport when he was 70, forty pounds overweight and had been given six months to live. At 88, he set a world age best for the marathon and ran, cycled and lifted weights until his death at 96.

Aristotle's proclamation that 'life is motion' would doubtless elicit a response from this new breed that 'motion is life'.

'Second Half' Recreation Programme

There is no reason why your sports ministry can't embrace and develop this group within your year round programme. There will, of course, be programming implications peculiar to these folk that need your careful consideration:

- They will respond to new challenges.
- They want to be fit and healthy.
- They are looking for meaning and purpose in life.
- They will have within their ranks tremendous

and varied giftings that can help to expand your ministry.

- They will be reliable and regular.
- They will be financially independent and supportive where expenses are required for kit, facilities, etc.
- They will have a strong network of close friends.
- They will vary from 'stay-at-homers' to those who want the ultimate challenge.

It is important, therefore, that what you offer is a new and innovative sports ministry approach to a group that is closer to heaven than most, but planning to delay their trip for as long as possible.

A group that is closer to heaven than most, but planning to delay their trip for as long as possible

SCOPE OF THE PROGRAMME

'Retired' is not a biblical term and has no place in the life of a Christian. Re-directed is a worthy substitute, as demonstrated in the life of Caleb, who, at the age of 85, asked God to 'give me this hill country' (Joshua 14:12). With this challenge ringing in our ears, let's look at the varied programme a church can offer in serving this 'transformation' age group.

- *Competitive team sports*: whatever the level of fitness, the muscles at this age take longer to recover from sustained activity and don't deal as well with quick movements as they used to do. The danger is for your mind to arrange an appointment that your body can't keep! We all like to think that we move at the speed of

The danger is for your mind to arrange an appointment that your body can't keep!

former years and are capable of doing the same tricks. For all these reasons, a lot of care needs to be taken over involving second half folk in competitive team sports. There will usually be a 'Stanley Matthews type' – played top level league football at 50 – who belies his age and can hold his place with those who are twenty years his junior but, by and large, any regular activity involving the majority from this grouping should be of a modified fashion, e.g. senior five-a-side football on a small pitch, touch rugby, crown green bowls, short-mat bowls, table-tennis and cricket. Cricket is a particularly good competitive sport for playing well into your sixties.

- *Competitive individual sports*: this area offers a wide range of possibilities such as swimming, tennis, squash, badminton and golf. Tournament ladders and ongoing competitions will be attractive to some. Pairings can be by age group or ability. Golf is a particular favourite, and some churches may see value in encouraging a number of 'second halfers' to take the game up and involve their friends at the same time. As a sport, it comes high on the list of friendship evangelism strategy.
- *Recreational sports*: these would be seen more in a social context and could be by team or individual. They would involve a lot of the activities named above but without the edge of sharp competition. Table games such as snooker, billiards, pool and table tennis fit into this category, as does tenpin bowling.

- *Wilderness/outdoor activities*: a whole variety of activities present themselves in this section. Hiking, walking, backpacking, camping, fishing, sailing, canoeing and skiing are ones that come to mind. Rambling weekends and walking retreats can be occasions when deep relationships are formed and the Christian life is actively role modeled.
- *Health and Fitness*: this is possibly the area that interests second half folk the most. Any church running its own health and fitness programme would have no difficulty recruiting this age group from inside and outside its precinct. Because it is such a key area, I shall endeavour to expand my thinking regarding its implications.

There are basically three components to be considered for a complete conditioning programme:

1. Endurance exercise (cardiovascular/aerobic)
2. Strength work
3. Stretching activities

With age, there is a natural deterioration of muscles and bones as well as the inevitable loss of aerobic and cardiovascular power. With 10 per cent loss of muscle mass every decade, after reaching 50 there is a real need to combat these areas of attrition.

JUST DO IT

For a number of years now, Anne Glover has run an aerobics/fitness programme at her church, Church Lane Evangelical, Stafford, for those over sixty and in their seventies and eighties. Her midweek session in the church hall also includes lunch, creative activities and Alpha courses. Many unchurched folk have attended these over the years and have become assimilated into the life of the fellowship as a consequence. Church holidays and weekends away regularly include those from the fitness group, and one year the holiday on the south coast of England carried an Olympic theme for the week!

ENDURANCE EXERCISE

The medical recommendation of 20–30 minute aerobic activity three times a week is a good guide for cardiovascular fitness. Brisk walking, jogging, cycling and swimming are the key activities here and should get the participant into the breathless zone with some sustained effort. Many find a regular regime of aerobic exercise difficult to maintain on their own and would welcome a weekly church activity that served this purpose. The devotional part of the activity could be planned to suit the group that is being served. To then encourage all members of the group to start their day with a thirty-minute brisk walk would be an added bonus to their conditioning programme. Some individuals could also build up their friendship patterns by enrolling at the local health and fitness club. Such clubs are very conscious of this age group's desire to maintain good health patterns and have designer programmes to suit all levels of fitness.

STRENGTH WORK

If the church is to run its own fitness programme, then a qualified instructor would be the first essential. Next to check on is the insurance cover for such activities in the church facility or hired premises. Training an instructor for this ministry is money well spent.

Training an instructor for this ministry is money well spent

Strength exercises can be

better performed on weight machines in the local leisure centre – two twenty-minute sessions per week would be ideal. However, a strength circuit can easily be devised in your church hall to include:

- sit ups (fingers touch tops of bent knees)
- squats (keep heels on ground and back straight)
- press ups (straight body, nose close to ground level)
- biceps curls (hand weights or bags of sugar)
- triceps push ups (hands behind you and on a bench – push up from there)

All these can be performed without equipment, apart from biceps curls, which need small hand weights. Individuals can then be encouraged to follow their own daily routine. A set of hand weights can easily be purchased at the local sports shop in whatever weight is required.

STRETCHING ACTIVITIES

These are pretty vital if you are to prevent future back and joint complaints. Any church fitness activity should always start with a gentle warm up and end with a cool down of stretching activities. Present physical educationalists have differing views regarding warm ups, but I always feel that the more you can inform your body that a change of pattern is coming, the better it will react to the session. Any fitness book on your local bookseller's shelves will give you a range of stretching exercises you can do from your neck to your toes. Observing how a cat stretches is a good guide for starting your day as you stretch your body lying on the ground by reaching to the extremities with your hands and your feet. Then, pushing your back gently into the floor will help to drain away any tension. Turning onto your front and doing the superman exercise will do wonders for your lower back, i.e. as you lift your right arm, lift your left leg at the same time, then reverse the procedure with left arm and right leg. Ten repetitions of each at a steady pace would be a good daily exercise for the back.

As you get older, it makes sense to concentrate even more heavily on a strength programme

As you get older, it makes sense to concentrate even more heavily on a strength programme. Half your fitness time should be spent on exercises that will build up your muscles and bones, since your vulnerability to the loss of these tissues becomes a looming threat as your years advance. Small weights with low repetitions are always a good place to start and any fitness centre will help you devise an appropriate programme.

Temple of the Holy Spirit

The Apostle Paul makes reference to the body as the 'temple of the Holy Spirit' (1 Corinthians 6:19) and the 'temple of the living God' (2 Corinthians 6:16). He was aware of the need for the church to preach good stewardship of the body as well as of finances and time. A sport and recreation ministry with folk in the second half of their lives reaches deep into this concept and should be married with the spiritual journey that is in progress.

Two spiritual notables, John Wesley and C.S. Lewis, were only too well aware of this necessary balance all men and women require in their lives. Wesley's four-point plan was recorded in his journal for his eighty-fifth year as being the reason why he had enjoyed such a long and energetic life:

1. Safeguard your daily devotion to God and make it part of your lifestyle.
2. Exercise regularly and seek a change of air.
3. Keep regular sleeping hours.
4. Be effective in managing stress.

C.S. Lewis, Christian writer and Oxbridge don, was a great walker who enjoyed sharing his walks with others and carrying out stimulating conversations with them. This is a great lesson to us all, because one of the best motivations for keeping going on an exercise programme is to find a companion whose company you enjoy and who makes you look forward to each session. If this person is one who does not yet know Christ in his life, then this can be an even greater motivation to maintain healthy exercise.

Walk and Don't be Faint (Isaiah 40:31)

The greatest and most achievable activity for the individual in the second half of life is undoubtedly that of walking. It is quietly becoming the most popular form of exercise in the UK, with fitness experts and doctors recommending it more than any other form of exercise. It lowers the risk of heart attack, stroke, high blood pressure and a whole host of other preventable diseases. It is an exercise that can be done on your own, with a companion or in a large group, and one that is always worth the effort. For the one who is doubtful about starting a walking programme, the reminder of an old Chinese proverb is challenging: 'A journey of a thousand miles begins with a single footstep'.

Jesus was a great walker and fulfilled much of his ministry

on the move. He taught his companions through stories and actions, often stopping to encourage, heal and teach many along the way. With his core team, he was able to section off quality time as they spent hours together on the dusty roads. Many of those conversations were so significant to the hearers that we have them recorded for our benefit in the gospels. Walking still allows opportunities for sharing our lives just as it did all those years ago in Palestine.

Walking has a high profile in the whole of the scriptures

Walking has a high profile in the whole of the scriptures. The Hebrew word for walk, *halak*, occurs more than 1,500 times in the Old Testament, and there are countless recordings of the Greek word for walk, *peripateo*, in the New Testament. Both words mean much more than the act of physical movement, rather, alluding to an individual's lifestyle or spiritual journey.

Walking offers opportunities for prayer that are not so easy with other physical exercises. An individual can go through his prayer list as he steps it out, two people can share and then pray for one another as they wander through the countryside, and a whole church group can prayer walk in their neighbourhood by praying for the occupants of each house as they pass by.

WHY WALK?

Most healthy people can significantly improve their cardiovascular fitness in just twelve weeks with a thoughtful objective-based walking programme. Three objectives should be basic to any scheme:

1. An increase in your overall distance.
2. An increase in the amount of time spent walking.
3. An increase in the speed you walk at.

Walking is so effective at burning calories that it can actually produce weight loss with no dieting at all. Walking a mile at a brisk pace burns up around a hundred calories, a similar rate per mile to jogging. A slower pace does not mean less benefit, only that it takes a bit longer to chalk up the calorie total.

Walking can be so easily achieved and is more acceptable to millions who would have no interest in more strenuous activities. The drop out rate as a consequence is negligible.

Dr Ken Cooper has highlighted four key times of the day for exercise: early morning, lunch, before the evening meal and at least one and a half hours after the evening meal. He recommends the early morning time for the reason that walkers are more likely to stick to their exercise habit because they are not faced with having to postpone it when unexpected events occur during the day.

BRISK WALKING

Where fitness is the primary goal, brisk walking rather than strolling is the recommended activity. The speed range runs from around twelve to twenty minutes per mile – three to five miles every hour. The slow end of this schedule produces many health benefits and the fast end produces a significant aerobic workout. Most healthy walkers should be able to operate at the pace of thirteen to fifteen minutes every mile, which would get their heart well into the target zone for fat burning and cardiovascular improvement.

Good upright posture, straight legs and a bent arm swing are the necessary ingredients for stride lengthening and speed increase. A stronger pumping action with the arms and a greater drive with the legs will raise the heart rate and improve the time.

Finally, any exercise regime will be more effective if walking is supplemented with strength training. More muscle results in a greater calorie burn even when you are resting. This is because muscle is more metabolically active and adding two pounds of muscle weight will result in around 120–140 calories being burnt every day. For suitable strength exercises, refer back to the earlier section in this chapter on 'strength work'.

To enter the second half of life is a challenging occasion. If a sport and recreation programme can refresh and renew this age group in both body and spirit, then it will be responsible for lives that are richer, fuller and more in tune with the God of the Universe. The prophet Jeremiah reminded his readers of this great quest when he recorded these visionary words: 'Ask where the good way is, and walk in it' (Jeremiah 6:16).

CHAPTER 9

Follow-up and Discipleship

Disciplemaking is the logical and caring thing to do with new Christians.
Christopher B. Adsit

In many ways, sport provides the ideal environment for leading people to Christ and then training them as disciples. Those you meet will generally enjoy company, be outgoing and open to life sharing. The problem with sports ministry in many churches is that it does a good job with sports, but rarely makes the transition to ministry. Organizing activities solely to make relationships is good up to a point. Any programme needs to include times where the Christian message is spelt out and the way is made clear for the participants to receive Christ for themselves. Otherwise, there is no difference between the church activity and the sports club down the road. The plus factor of the Cross must underpin all your plans and aspirations.

I remember many years ago benefiting as a student from the ministry of the Navigators and their remarkable attention to detail in discipleship training. The new Christian was always encouraged to spend a good year with the person who had led him to Christ so they could pray and read the Bible together and help each other on to Christian maturity in the lifestyle they shared. Jesus himself gave so much attention to discipleship that he spent three very full years building into the lives of men and women who were to advance the kingdom of God to its next stage. He knew the value of having a small detachment of believers taught to be prayer warriors, soaked in scriptural truth and obedient to the leading of the Holy Spirit. It wasn't surprising that they gained a reputation for turning the world upside down.

The success of the Alpha Course over the last decade in introducing vast numbers of people to the claims of Christ and the life changing power of the Holy Spirit has been largely due to the convivial atmosphere created in a non-threatening environment. Alpha has allowed its participants to absorb ideas, voice their thoughts and observe Christ in the lives of others. In similar fashion, a sport and recreation programme should have inbuilt into it an 'Investigating Christian Belief' course that is user-friendly to sports people. This means that any presentation of the gospel can be followed by an invitation to enquirers to join the course. The following 'Race of Life' study is an example of a four-week course that would take such enquirers through the basic foundations of the Christian life and provide them with the opportunity to come to faith themselves. Each week requires a little background reading on the part of the participant, so that a mixture of sharing and teaching can take place. The material is such that it can be covered adequately in one hour. Organizing a buffet style meal around the topic under discussion can only assist in the forging of relationships and the flow of conversation. Copies of the study booklet can be obtained from Christians in Sport.

In seeking to convince his readers of the refreshing challenge found in the Christian life, the Apostle Paul made frequent reference to 'running the race'. He encouraged the Christians at Philippi to keep their focus on 'what is ahead' as they 'pressed towards the goal' and sought to 'win the prize'. He believed there was a 'race marked out', a race both demanding and exciting, with a throbbing stadium beckoning the runners who completed the distance.

These studies consider what is required of the spiritual athlete in the RACE OF LIFE. The resurrection of Jesus is examined as the gateway into the RACE, together with other pre-race requisites. The investigator can study the role Jesus plays as confidant and coach and begin to understand something of the training schedule mapped out for the Christian athlete.

The investigator can study the role Jesus plays as confidant and coach

A final comparison with athletes who have 'completed the course' gives a true sense of both the challenge in starting the RACE and the eternal significance in finishing it.

Study 1 – The Race Conditions

'I press on towards the goal to win the prize'
Philippians 3:14

No serious athlete enters a race unless he knows what is required of him. A full investigation of the race conditions is called for. This is also the case with entry into the Kingdom of God.

The EVENTS surrounding the life of Jesus are both amazing and unique. God himself in the person of Jesus Christ stepped into human history. Much is at stake on the strength of this assertion and so it is vital for us to take a long and unbiased look at the surrounding facts.

RESURRECTION

Read some of the gospel accounts of the resurrection: John chapter 20 and Luke chapter 24.

How did different people react to the resurrection of Jesus?
See Matthew 28:1–15, Acts 5:25–32, Acts 17:16–23,32

Are there other possible explanations for the empty tomb?

BOTTOM LINE

Why do you think Christian belief hinges on the truth of the resurrection of Jesus?

What is your personal opinion at this stage?

RELIABLE OR WHAT?

The New Testament was written between AD 48 and AD 110. Records go back to as early as AD 120 and are found in over 4,000 Greek texts and many more are found in other ancient languages. By comparison, the details of Caesar's Gallic Wars (58 BC–50 BC) are only found in a handful of manuscripts, the earliest of which was written around AD 900. No keen scholar of history would doubt the authenticity of the latter!

A FURTHER QUESTION . . .

Can I be sure that the New Testament writers were telling the truth and had not been deceived by the lies of others?

Investigate their statements and claims:

Luke 1:1–4

Comment...

2 Peter 1:16
Comment...

The Apostle Paul had a life changing experience when he had a personal encounter with Jesus Christ. It led him to assert, 'Jesus Christ, declared with power to be the Son of God by his resurrection from the dead' (Romans 1:4).

CONCLUSION

If Jesus rose from the dead and he is still alive today, then it must be possible for us to know him. The next study examines closely how this relationship can be forged.

Study 2 – Beginning the Race

'Let us fix our eyes on Jesus, the author and perfector of our faith' *Hebrews 12:2*

The point of entry into the Christian life starts with the RACE OF LIFE. Jesus is exceptionally qualified to be the STARTER of the RACE.

Discuss the following statements:

- He has experienced the RACE for himself (Hebrews 12:2).
- He knows intimately all the pitfalls (Hebrews 4:15).
- Only he knows the way to the stadium (John 14:6).
- He will be at the finishing tape (Philippians 3:14).

Once we begin to accept the claims Jesus made about himself, we then hit stormy weather concerning his death.

WHY DID HE HAVE TO DIE?

1. It was part of God's plan
 Examine 1 Peter 1:10–12 and Hebrews 1:1–2

'But you Bethlehem Ephrathah, though you are small among the clans of Judah, out of you will come for me one who will be ruler over Israel, whose origins are from old, from ancient times'.
Micah 5:2 (prophet, 700 BC approx.)

2. Jesus predicted it.
 See Mark 9:30–32

What did Jesus chose to do?
John 10:17–18

3. It was God's way of rescuing mankind.
Read 1 Peter 3:18
What did Jesus die for?
Who did Jesus die for?
What was the result of his death?

Our RACE entry form has been signed by Jesus. Without his sacrifice, we are ineligible to compete (1 John 5:12).

IS IT TIME TO START THE RACE?

The Bible gives four steps you must consider:

A. Admit you are a sinner and have a need of God (Romans 3:23)
B. Believe (trust) in Jesus Christ (Romans 10:9)
C. Consider the relative costs and the rewards (John 3:16 & Luke 8:34,35)

D. Do it! . . . Decide to put Jesus first in your life (John 1:12)

You could say a prayer like this:

'Lord Jesus Christ
I know I have sinned in my thoughts, words and actions.
There are so many good things I have not done.
Please forgive me and help me to turn from everything I know to be wrong.
You gave your life on the cross for me and now I gladly give my life to you.
Come in to be my Saviour, Lord and friend and fill me now with your Spirit.
Amen'

You have now started the Race of Life. Never doubt the day Jesus started you off. There will be tough days ahead, but Jesus promises to be your constant running companion (Hebrews 13:5 & 13:8).

Enjoy the RUN . . . there is a great finish!

Study 3 – The Training Programme

'Everyone who competes in the games goes into strict training' *1 Corinthians 9:25*

Jesus Christ can enter your life and forgive you immediately, but it will take a lifetime for your character to be transformed 'into his likeness' (Philippians 2:5).

The dedicated athlete knows that an all year round training programme is essential for peak fitness. The Christian athlete must seek to keep his spiritual life in the fitness zone where it will grow strong and healthy. Consider five areas where the 'disciple' (a learner in training) can make good progress in his spiritual fitness.

1. KEEP UP THE INTAKE LEVEL (BIBLE STUDY)

Discuss how 2 Timothy 3:16 can be fully implemented.

2. BE A GOOD TEAM PLAYER (FELLOWSHIP)

a) What did Jesus have to say about our relationships with others? (John 13:34,35)

b) Might there be some adjustments in priorities? (Philippians 2:3,4)

c) Why is it so important to meet with other believers? (Hebrews 10:24,25)

3. PLAY UP FRONT (TELLING OTHERS)

Simon of Cyrene identified with Jesus in the public place (Luke 23:26). How can Christians take up the cross and follow Jesus? (Romans 1:16)
Why might you be ashamed of being a Christian?

4. COMMUNICATE REGULARLY WITH THE COACH (PRAYER)

Look at Philippians 4:6,7.
What does this mean on a daily basis?

5. DO THE BUSINESS ON MATCH DAY (ACHIEVING GOALS)

Consider what bearing fruit involves (John 15:8). Very few athletes manage to remain at the top by relying on natural ability only. A disciplined approach to training is vital. Getting the pulse rate into the target zone at regular intervals has many benefits.

- It increases the blood supply to the muscles.
- It increases the number of blood capillaries around the heart, thereby strengthening it.
- It increases the aerobic capacity of the body.

In the same way, the spiritual athlete needs to 'breathe in' the presence of God (Bible study, prayer, fellowship, faith-sharing) at regular intervals in order to keep his 'heart' (inner being) in God's target zone.
What benefits do you think can come from this?

Study 4 – Maintaining the Pace

'Run with perseverance the race marked out' *Hebrews 12:1*

Many talented athletes have not made the grade because their skill level was not matched by determination and endurance. Many aspire, few attain! The Tokyo-produced documentary of Abibe Bikila's Marathon victory in the 1964 Olympics was a case in point. The camera closely followed the Ethiopian for every step of his journey and clearly illustrated the discipline required to cope with all aspects of the race. By contrast, other athletes were seen sitting down at the drinks station and obtaining lifts back to the stadium.

What does the Bible have to say about maintaining pace in the Christians life?
Philippians 3:12–14
Hebrews 12:1–3
Hebrews 12:7,12

Discuss what obstacles you are likely to encounter as you press on in the Christian faith (Hebrews 3:12).

Eric Liddell, in the film *Chariots of Fire* is remembered for his dedication to the spiritual race as well as the physical one (gold medal in the 1924 Olympics for the 400 metres and rugby union caps for Scotland as a winger). What many do not know is that he ended his life in a Japanese internment camp where his love and care for others belied his own physical hardships. As a dedicated spiritual athlete, he continued to rise before dawn and meet with his eternal coach. He had the stadium in his sights and he was not going to falter.

Consider the RACE that Abraham ran in Hebrews 11:8–10.
How did it start?
Where was the course?
What was his race attitude?
Where was he heading for?

What encourages the spiritual athlete daily in his relationship with Jesus Christ, his personal coach? (Revelation 21:5–7)

Review
Record three things about the RACE OF LIFE that you believe God has spoken to you about during these studies:

1 ....
2 ....
3 ....

Remember, Jesus runs with you . . . always (Matthew 28:20).

There is little doubt that a sport and recreation programme will make inroads into any local community in ways no other church programme can achieve. Many American churches would attribute their quantum growth leaps to the success of their sports ministry. My visit to Willow Creek Church near Chicago in Illinois in the late 90s revealed a sports department that had 122 basketball teams operating in their inter-mural league. The programme was for the men of the church and their friends and sought to transport the players from the gymnasium to the sanctuary through friendship evangelism. It may seem an obvious point to make, but sports ministry must be geared to men and women, boys and girls being reborn into God's Kingdom. It is then that the fun starts.

A sport and recreation programme will make inroads into any local community in ways no other church programme can achieve

Taking a new Christian through to mature discipleship is not a strategy that the local church always has high on its list. Fortunately, it was high on Jesus' list, and became a vital part of his final instructions to his disciples as they were clearly told to 'go and make disciples' throughout the world. They had Jesus as a role model and from the word 'go' gave close attention to nurturing individual growth.

The methodology of discipleship is all important, and in this respect certain statistics can be quite staggering. Should an evangelist reach one person a day, then 11,680 people would be reached in 32 years. If each new discipler trains one person a year to become a discipler himself, then the number grows to 4,294,967,296 in the same period of time.

The sports ministry environment provides the ideal setting for discipleship training. To play a part in leading someone

The sports ministry environment provides the ideal setting for discipleship training

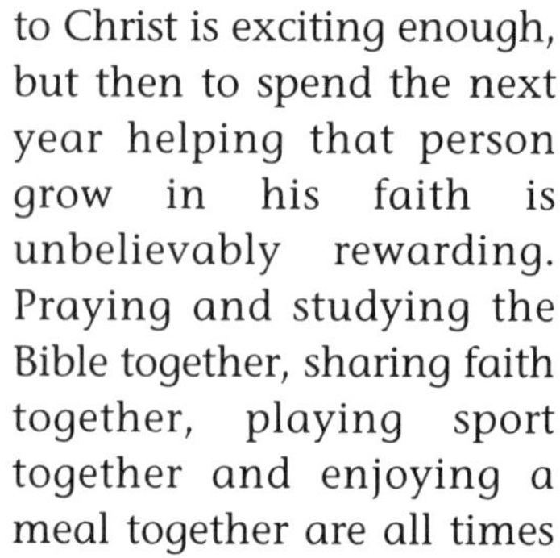

to Christ is exciting enough, but then to spend the next year helping that person grow in his faith is unbelievably rewarding. Praying and studying the Bible together, sharing faith together, playing sport together and enjoying a meal together are all times when the disciple learns the rudiments of becoming a mature believer in Christ and playing a part in bringing others to that same point. Indeed, the two goals of discipleship would be for the disciple to become a 'self-feeder' and then a 'reproducer'.

Discipleship Strategy

Like any effective sports ministry programme, discipleship planning and strategy does not happen naturally. It requires prayer and practical design. The potential to teach, train and transmit within an environment that is Christ centred cannot be over emphasized. The teaching moments can make reality out of theory with spiritual analogies from everyday sporting activities. Training consists of instruction that can then be repeated and reinforced through regular contact together. Finally, there is the challenging responsibility of demonstrating the Christian life. In many ways, the discipler's attitude on the field of play and in pressure situations can have a greater influence than the day's Bible study together. To see the 'walk' match the 'talk' can often be the breakthrough time for the disciple.

The world of sport and recreation is a great instructional area for the fresh disciple. There is so much in the rules and the manner of sport that can be looked at parabolically, as earthly situations are seen in the light of heavenly meanings. Paul the Apostle moved in a Greek society that focused a lot of its attention on physical fitness and games competitions. Like Jesus before him, Paul took the interests of the day and used them as a platform for instruction. Sport itself provides a spiritual laboratory for the Christian participant, where the trying and testing of faith is an ongoing process. Spiritual progress, or lack of it, can often be measured by reaction and temperament on the sports field and the discipleship situation is the ideal place to address both. To be able to put failure to live up to God's standards against the backcloth of 2 Timothy 3:16 ('teaching, rebuking, correcting and training in righteousness') is an important part of the process of growth. However, perhaps the greatest area of instruction for the new disciple is that of personal accountability. The writer of Proverbs gives helpful advice when he notes that 'wounds from a friend can be trusted' (Proverbs 27:6) and 'as iron sharpens iron, so one man sharpens another' (Proverbs 27:17). To be prepared to let another watch your back and comment on the most personal and sensitive of issues is also to let the Holy Spirit instruct your innermost character.

The final part of the discipleship strategy is that of modelling and mentoring. As Jesus moved around Galilee, he was incarnational, not informational. He didn't bring news from heaven: he brought heaven itself down to the lives of men and women. If you wanted to know about God, you looked at Jesus and saw how he dealt with people and safeguarded his time with his Heavenly Father.

Once you are living the gospel, then it becomes such a short step to inspire others with its message

The discipler has got to live the Christian life knowing that his friends will take their cue from what they see of God in him. Once you are living the gospel, then it becomes such a short step to inspire others with its message.

I owe a lot to the Navigator organization for its discipleship programme in my own life as a young teacher. The building blocks of Bible study, prayer, fellowship and witnessing were constantly impressed, repeated and reinforced in my life, and are the foundations that I am still able to stand upon. What an impact would be felt in the community if sports ministry disciples from the local church systematically sought to disciple others in the ways of God. Then God's Kingdom would be seen to be growing at a pace.

Bibliography

Cooper, Dr Kenneth, *The Aerobics Way*, Transworld Publishers, 1978

Cooper, Dr Kenneth, *Faith-Based Fitness*, Thomas Nelson Publishers, 1997

Guiness, Os, *The Call*, Authentic Lifestyle, 2001

Kingsley, Charles, *Health and Education*, 1874

Ladd, Tony, & Mathisen, James, *Muscular Christianity*, Baker Book House, 1999

Linville, Dr Greg, *The Theology of Competition*, Overwhelming Victory Ministries

MacDonald, Gordon, *Ordering Your Private World*, Highland Books, 1985

Maxwell, Jim, *Body and Soul*, New Hope Publishers, 2000

Oswald, Rodger, *Sports Ministry and the Church*, Church Sports International

Weir, Stuart, *More than Champions*, Zondervan, 1993

Weir, Stuart, *What the Book Says About Sport*, Bible Reading Fellowship, 2000

Wilson, Julian, *Complete Surrender*, Monarch Publications, 1996

Easy Find Index

(sports ministry activities highlighted for quick reference purposes)

Christians in Sport

Christians in Sport is a missionary organization with a vision to '**reach the world of sport for Christ**' and exists to share the great news about Jesus with boys, girls, men and women who have been given sporting talents by God and who invest much of their physical and mental energy in playing, coaching and officiating in the world of sport at all levels from the young novice to the professional international athlete.

As an organization we yearn that every Christian involved in sport in the United Kingdom might see that they can make a difference for Christ amongst their friends and colleagues by the intentional investment of their prayers and practice. We would love to see a Christian in every place or institution where sport is played, coached or administered.

There can be no doubt that sport is a global phenomenon. It doesn't matter whether you are in the UK or the USA, Calcutta or Coventry, people play, watch and talk about sport in their millions every day. It is the largest people group on earth and one that has its own universal language. Within this vast group **Christians in Sport** works with professionals, players, churches, university students and young people. In all these areas we are determined to equip and train all those who are serious about their Christian faith and their sport. If you come into this category then it would be our joy to work with you.

Professionals and Players. Working primarily through staff, fieldworkers, chaplains and volunteers to encourage those who play sport – whether professionals, adult players, students, teenagers or recreational players – to see their team or club as their mission field.

Churches. Envisioning and equipping churches to realize the potential of sport and recreation in building relationships with those within their communities.

Game of Two Halves (GO2H). A Christians in Sport project in association with Tearfund aimed at placing social action on the agenda of the sports world.

Academy. An accredited training course in partnership with All Nations Christian College, designed to equip practically and theologically workers for the mission field of the sports world.

International. Encouraging the development of indigenous sports ministries around the world through shared knowledge, experience and resources.

Major Sports Event Outreach. Seeking to resource the Christian community both in the UK and abroad with quality evangelistic resources, particularly relating to major sports events.

Ongoing development of the above is regularly communicated and illustrated via Christians in Sport's quarterly magazine.

If you want to know more about the work of **Christians in Sport** and how you can get involved then please don't hesitate to contact us. We'll be delighted to hear from you.

Christians in Sport
Frampton House
Victoria Road
BICESTER OX26 2GA

Tel: 01869 255630
Fax: 01869 255640
Email: info@christiansinsport.org.uk
Website: www.christiansinsport.org.uk

Church Sports and Recreation Ministers

HELPING SPORTS MINISTERS REACH THE WORLD

- CSRM is an organization that helps Sports and Recreation Ministers in the local church and those working in specialized sports ministries reach the world for Christ.
- CSRM is an organization that facilitates a network of sports and recreation ministry professionals within the worldwide church of Christ.
- CSRM is Christ centered, biblically based, evangelistically focused, international in scope and ecumenical in participation

History. CSRM was incorporated in 1995, emerging from a grass roots movement which began in 1990. It was created to provide a professional organization for those seeking to use sports and recreation as a tool for evangelism and discipleship within the local church. It currently serves over 700 churches and many specialized sports ministries. Members can be found in countries from around the world and is open to any sports and recreation minister and even those training future sports ministers. While voting members come from local churches, any sports minister can become a member. Members are found in Japan, Africa, England, Australia, India, Canada and many other countries.

Conferences. CSRM sponsors an annual conference at a local church for anyone interested in sport and recreation ministry and has also developed an international network of regional conferences being held in different countries. For the latest conference information contact the CSRM website – www.csrm.org.

Journal. CSRM publishes a quarterly journal *The Sports Minister*, which keeps its membership up to date with training options, conference information, regional gatherings and job opportunities. It also serves as a repository of cutting edge research, programming ideas, past and current sports ministry history and all CSRM business.

Website. The website (www.csrm.org) gives CSRM the technological ability to communicate the same type of information as is found in *The Sports Minister* and is an important 'up to the minute' link for those seeking employment or employees within the field of sports ministry. It also includes sections for accessing sports ministry resources, a speakers' bureau and all educational institutions that teach sports ministry.

Training. CSRM has consulted with Christian Colleges and Seminaries in different countries to help them develop a curriculum for church recreation and sports ministry in general. In addition CSRM board members regularly teach classes and have served as adjunct professors at several schools. For a list of all known schools with sports ministry classes consult the website – www.csrm.org. CSRM has developed a systematic training track that will enhance sports and recreation ministries in the local church. This is an internationally recognized certification.

Consulting. The CSRM Executive Director is available to local churches, other ministries and conferences for consultations. Many current and former board members are also available.

For more information contact:

Dr Greg Linville – Executive Director
C/O The World Outreach Center
5350 Broadmoor Circle N.W.
Canton, OH 44709
USA

Tel: 330-493-4824
Fax: 330-493-0852
www.csrm.org